THE

FISCAL

CLIFF

HOW AMERICA CAN AVOID A FALL AND STAY ON TOP

INTRODUCTION BY BRIAN BAKER,
PRESIDENT OF ENDING SPENDING

AYŞE İMROHOROĞLU, PHD, AND
SELAHATTIN İMROHOROĞLU, PHD

TABLE OF
CONTENTS

I want to make America fiscally safe and secure for generations to come.

I believe that when it comes to the most vital issues our nation faces, Americans need to stay informed, reach conclusions, and let themselves be heard (whether by voting or otherwise).

I also believe that our country's debt-to-GDP ratio is a more important indicator of the condition of our overall economy than a price-to-earnings ratio is for a publicly traded company.

With these ideas in mind, last year I set out to find a top-notch economist who could simply, effectively (and quantitatively) describe the financial debacle facing America.

I found two top-notch economists, a husband-wife team—both professors at the University of Southern California and experts on a range of America's most critical macroeconomic issues. I asked them to write a book so that policy makers (and people like myself) could better understand America's ticking fiscal time bomb.

But then I asked for more: "I want you not only to explain America's current financial crisis but to give me a practical solution."

And they did.

Their solution is a little different from what I had expected. But as I read their detailed evidence and studied their impartial arguments, I realized that their verdict (tough, fair, unvarnished) provides a clear path forward, a path to prosperity that I hope is the legacy from my generation to those who follow.

Sincerely,

Joe Ricketts
ENTREPRENEUR

INTRODUCTION

S ince the Founding Fathers, the politics of drafting America's federal budget has always been among the most complex and divisive issues our elected representatives face. This is understandable; when we set a budget, we determine our national priorities and grapple with the thorny question of how to pay for those priorities. Thus, a budget is a moral document, a reflection of our national purpose that allocates resources among competing demands and helps to determine how much money should be collected from the people in the form of taxes. When we understand it in that framework, we can see why partisans on both sides care so deeply, and fight so hard, to advance their views.

It is also why many Americans may be shocked to learn that those who serve as our lawmakers are, in fact, breaking the law. The Congressional Budget Act of 1974 establishes a specific timetable for the congressional budget process and requires, among other things, that Congress complete action on a concurrent resolution of the federal budget by April 15 of each year. Despite that legal requirement—and the obvious fact that passing a budget is the most basic obligation of Congress—we have had no actual federal budget for the past few years. In 2010, for the first time since the adoption of the Budget Act of 1974, the House of Representatives failed to pass a budget resolution. And, as of the publication date of this book, the Senate has not passed a budget in over 1,000 days—more than three years!

For his part, President Barack Obama has submitted budget proposals to Congress every year he has been in office. Yet in 2011 the Senate unanimously rejected the president's last two annual budget proposals, and in 2012, the House unanimously rejected the president's 2013 budget.

The only budget that has passed either chamber of Congress in the past two years is the budget introduced by House Budget Committee Chairman Rep. Paul Ryan, yet a closely divided Senate also rejected that budget plan. Finally, Congress has not passed all of the necessary appropriations (or spending) bills prior to the start of the government's fiscal year since 1996, which further imperils the proper functioning of our national government. Clearly, the budget process is broken.

The failure of the Senate to pass a budget resolution is an abdication of responsibility on the part of our nation's leaders. The consequences are dire. In the absence of a budget agreed to by a majority of our nation's leaders, our nation simply spends without direction or limit. And, as this book makes clear, even when we have had a budget, our government has refused to restrain spending.

Many Americans observe the annual budget fights warily, wishing that both sides would just "get along." However, the simple fact that something is bipartisan does not necessarily mean it will produce a good result for the American people. After all, it was a bipartisan addiction to spending that helped dig the $15 trillion hole we are in.

The numbers speak for themselves, and demonstrate that Washington has a serious spending problem. According to budget tables from the Office of Management and Budget, total federal spending has increased 62% faster than inflation since 2000. In fact, by comparing the total outlays in 2000 ($2.29 trillion) with those in 2010 ($3.72 trillion), we see that total federal spending increased by $1.43 trillion over that 10-year period. While those numbers include the tremendous costs of fighting two wars and the rapid increase in health care entitlement spending, there has also been a dramatic growth in nondefense discretionary spending. In fact, nondefense discretionary spending was $522.4 billion in fiscal year 2008 and climbed to $658.2 billion in fiscal year 2010. That is a 26% increase.

Overall, federal spending as a percentage of the economy is now slightly more than 24%, well above the historic average of 18-20%. This means that roughly one of every four dollars generated by working Americans is taxed and spent by our federal government.

Of course, not every dollar that is spent is raised in tax revenue, so we have deficits. Indeed, for four straight years, the federal government's annual budget deficit—the difference between how much the government raised in taxes and how much it spent on programs—has exceeded $1 trillion each year. This translates to a startling fact: the government is forced to borrow 42 cents of every dollar that it spends.

All of this deficit spending is how we have accumulated our $15 trillion national debt. Consider that the debt rose by a total of $4.89 trillion during George W. Bush's eight-year presidency, and, as of April 2012, the debt had increased by an additional $5 trillion during the first three years of President Obama's term.

These alarming figures are symptoms of fundamental underlying problems: our government is too big, spends too much, and does too many things for too many people (with too few to actually pay for it). This unsustainable growth in government spending is pushing the nation toward the edge of a fiscal cliff that could mean a steep fall into a debt-fueled economic crisis, threatening our national survival and the prosperity of all Americans, especially the less fortunate.

In the pages that follow, the authors analyze and diagnose our fiscal challenges in much greater detail. The question confronting us is: What can we do about it? While this is a daunting challenge, we must all remember that balancing the budget is possible. In fact, it was not so long ago that a president of one party (Clinton) worked together with congressional leaders of the opposition party (Dole and Gingrich) to balance the budget.

For starters, we must understand the political problems in Washington. Far too many of our political leaders are more worried about the next election than the next generation. In order to change this dynamic, we, the people, must demand that our elected officials take seriously their legal and moral obligations to adopt a credible budget plan. To me, this means a budget that is balanced (where the government incurs no further debt) and includes a provision to pay down the debt already owed. Now, this isn't to suggest that there are no officials in Congress who have been willing to discuss the problems with our debt; there certainly are. Yet for doing so, these legislators have been subjected to criticism from members of the opposition party, or even from their own political party. A bipartisan roster of leaders like Republicans John Boehner, Paul Ryan, and Jim DeMint and Democrats Ron Wyden, Dick Durbin, and Claire McCaskill, to name just a few, has had the courage to step forward. Our job as citizens is to require all of our elected officials to come together and solve this problem.

In the past few years, various groups have formed to study the coming debt crisis and offer solutions and recommendations as to how to solve it, including the Bipartisan Policy Center, the Peterson-Pew Commission on Budget Reform, and perhaps most notably, the National Commission on Fiscal Responsibility and Reform (established by President Obama and commonly known by the last names of the commission's two cochairs, Alan Simpson and Erskine Bowles). Additionally, several individual members of Congress and sometimes groups of members have introduced their own proposed budgets, including Representatives Paul Ryan, Jim Cooper, Steven LaTourette, and Chris Van Hollen, and Senators Tom Coburn, Mike Lee, Pat

Toomey, and Rand Paul. Of all these well-intentioned efforts, the two that have garnered the most attention from the American public are the Simpson-Bowles plan and the budget proposal offered by the House Budget Committee.

In order to understand the solution to the debt crisis, we must understand the principles underlying the work of the Simpson-Bowles plan. In short, the Simpson-Bowles Commission, comprising a bipartisan group of business, labor, and congressional leaders appointed by the president and Congress, reached a bipartisan consensus on a number of important points. These individuals recognized that our country needs spending restraint; significant reforms to our health and retirement security programs; and a simplified tax code oriented toward growth. The Simpson-Bowles Commission produced an outline, not written in legislative language, that was supported by 11 of 18 of its members. Ultimately, while it was heralded at the time, the Simpson-Bowles plan was ignored by the Obama administration. Indeed, in February 2011, just three months after the report was released, President Obama released his budget, which Simpson and Bowles said goes "nowhere near where they will have to go to resolve our fiscal nightmare."

Rep. Paul Ryan, chairman of the House Budget Committee and a member of the Simpson-Bowles Commission who dissented from the report but complimented it as a "comprehensive and credible plan for getting the federal government's fiscal house in order," introduced a budget in April 2011, which the House of Representatives later passed. (A similar, slightly modified version of this "House budget" also passed in 2012.) The House budget, which unlike Simpson-Bowles did not contain net tax increases, nevertheless built upon the work of the Simpson-Bowles Commission, with both Simpson and Bowles themselves stating that it represented a "serious, honest, straightforward approach to addressing our nation's enormous fiscal challenges."

Whatever plan is ultimately adopted by our government, it must reflect significant components of the Simpson-Bowles plan and the House budget in order to be successful. The principles underlying each of these budgets are sound for moving forward in a practical way. Spending restraint and fundamental entitlement and tax reform are the crucial ingredients of a debt solution.

While everyone understands the necessity of responsible spending restraint (whether implemented through a cap on total spending or mandatory across-the-board reductions), entitlement reform is a hot-button political issue. Yet, once the facts shown in this book are fully understood by the public, hopefully we can move forward to protect and strengthen the vital health and retirement security programs of Medicare, Medicaid, and Social Security. The facts are clear that exploding federal spending on health care programs is the primary driver of our long-term debt. Given the changing nature of demographics in our country, programs that were designed and implemented 60 to 80 years ago will simply not continue to work into the mid-21st century. What's more, the recent expansion of these entitlement programs will become even less affordable in the future, as changing demographics demand ever more cost increases. Any budget plan must include specific, structural reforms to Medicare and Medicaid, which will not only ensure benefits for current and future beneficiaries but will also help avert a looming and severe debt crisis.

The other key bipartisan consensus that has been reached is the need for fundamental tax reform. Our leaders have used the tax code to advance priorities, and thus the code is full of so-called tax expenditures (also known as the deductions and credits that many Americans have come to expect). But in the process, the tax system has become far too complex and difficult to navigate (and for some, easy to manipulate). Lowering tax rates and simplifying the tax code will generate greater revenue by spurring economic growth, especially if we do not increase the government's take from the economy.

Simply raising taxes is not enough to eliminate the deficit because, for starters, tax increases destroy the incentive to reduce spending and decrease the opportunity for economic growth.

Furthermore, while the vast majority of Americans do pay taxes, including payroll, state, and sales taxes (to name a few), a recent report from the Congressional Joint Committee on Taxation shows that 51% of households in America paid no federal income tax in 2009, even though they used programs funded by federal income tax revenues. Thus, an increasingly small group of citizens is paying an increasingly large share for the government benefits of all. By lowering rates, broadening the tax base, and adopting pro-growth policies, it is possible to increase revenue to the government while ensuring that all citizens pay their fair share.

Many who have studied this issue have noted that the coming debt crisis is the "most predictable crisis in history." Our generation's challenge is to figure out how to live within our means, and the answers to many of the key questions can be found in this book and the work of those who have studied the problem before us. We do not need yet another study or debt commission, because, as Sen. Tom Coburn has said so correctly, Congress is "the debt commission."

I encourage every American, once armed with the facts, to demand that your elected representatives change our country's course. To paraphrase Lincoln and Roosevelt, if we do not act now to balance the budget and pay down the debt, our nation will not and cannot long endure.

Brian C. Baker

PRESIDENT, ENDING SPENDING

CHAPTER 1

COMMON SENSE

America is in trouble.

Unless something is done promptly, the United States will soon face debt levels that are more than double their historical averages. But the real trouble lies in how America might try to reduce its debt. Relying heavily on tax increases will destroy what made America great: innovation, long-run growth, and a vibrant workforce. Only basic economic principles and bipartisan political leadership can save us. In this increasingly global and competitive 21st century, America needs to exercise some common sense.

This book will educate the reader on America's current fiscal problems and how these are likely to become considerably worse in the future. However, in the midst of rising debt and deficits lies a great opportunity for reform that is long overdue. This book suggests that the best, and perhaps the only, way out of our self-inflicted fiscal mess is to focus on two key economic principles:

1

• Eliminate tax deductions to increase government revenues, and lower income tax rates to promote job creation and growth.

• Reduce and reform government expenditures on public health care, Social Security, and other entitlement programs.

It's that simple.

To make this case, we will organize our book into three parts.
• First, we'll discuss the role of government in the economy (and our everyday lives) using simple economic logic and examples.

• Second, we'll describe how the U.S. government gets its revenue and spends its money, including the financial shortfalls that lead to additional federal debt (and the impact this has on the economy).

• Finally, we will revisit the two principles mentioned above, to consider the best path for achieving future fiscal balance.

The U.S. economy is slowly growing out of the Great Recession of 2007–2009, brought on by the financial crisis of 2007–2009. The unemployment rate is still quite high. Federal government debt held by the public was $10.127 trillion by the end of September 2011 (with intergovernmental holdings adding another $4.663 trillion). With a nominal gross domestic product (GDP) of $15.176 trillion for the same period, the debt-to-output ratio was 66.7% by the third quarter of 2011. This is nearly twice as high as the average debt-to-GDP ratio between 1960 and 2010. If America does not take serious precautions now, debt-to-GDP ratio will exceed 100% in 10 years, if not sooner. Indeed, according to some scenarios, debt-to-GDP may exceed 200% by 2021.

What is the big deal? Well, for most of the 1990s and 2000s, the Greek debt-to-GDP ratio stood at about 100%. In 2009, it jumped to 126.8%, and severe problems started. Greek bonds are currently in default (rated CC by Standard & Poor's), indicating little prospect for recovery. Despite the "haircuts" taken by the bondholders, Greek citizens are facing years of hardship to pay off the rest of their debt. Their economy is in disarray with little chance to show growth over the next few years. In fact, the Greek economy has been in a recession since 2008. The economy contracted 6.8% in 2010 and 3.5% in 2011 and is projected to decline 2.8% in 2012. There was a 27% increase in bankruptcies between 2010 and 2011. The unemployment rate was 19.9% in 2011, with a youth unemployment rate of 48%. In 2010, an adviser to then Prime Minister George Papandreou predicted that Greece's recovery from this crisis would take about 15 years.

The debt-to-GDP ratio is an instructive indicator for measuring the fiscal health of any country's economy, including America's.

The U.S. debt-to-GDP now stands at about 70%. It will rise above 80% by the end of 2012. More important, this rise is not expected to be temporary like wartime increases in debt.

If America does not curtail expenditures and find ways to enhance tax revenues, we are looking at a debt-to-GDP ratio over 100% by 2022, if not sooner. This prospect is ruining short-term growth possibilities by creating huge uncertainties in future business and consumer conditions. More important, it is threatening to derail America's long-run growth path. There is evidence that a debt-to-GDP ratio over 90% is associated with

1% lower growth per year. In 40 years, this results in a loss of nearly 50% of average household income relative to normal growth.

Through increased government revenue (by increasing the tax base) and reduced government spending (cuts to entitlements), the U.S. can bring debt-to-GDP to its historical average level of 40%. Only this will restore and reignite America's growth prospects for the long run. It is important to understand that even a one-percentage-point difference in growth rates over a long period of time accumulates, producing large differences in per capita income. For an American citizen with a $50,000 income in 2012, this presents a choice between $110,000 versus only $74,000 in 40 years.

Surprisingly, there is already a bipartisan blueprint that would accomplish this—the Moment of Truth report from the president's National Commission on Fiscal Responsibility and Reform (better known as the Simpson-Bowles plan). Only neither the president nor Congress, neither the Republicans nor the Democrats have the political courage (or conviction) to champion it.

By underscoring our two crucial economic principles, we are going to do just that . . . because it's common sense.

THE FISCAL CLIFF

CHAPTER 2

GOVERNMENT'S ROLE IN THE ECONOMY: A PRIMER

The recent turmoil in financial markets and the worldwide slowdown in economic activity have brought the role of government in the economy to the forefront of public discussion. Governments in the European Union, Japan, and the United States have adopted monetary (interest-rate) and fiscal (spending/tax) policies to stimulate their economies, which has provoked questions about the extent to which the public sector should be involved in the day-to-day management of an economy.

Given the renewed focus on government spending and taxation, what do economic theory and practice say about the role of government in the economy? Our goal is to address this question using publicly available data and simple economic insight.

The United States government (defined as federal, state, and local government):

- Imposes a range of taxes to finance public consumption and investment expenditures

- Pays interest on existing government debt

- Pays for social insurance programs such as Social Security, Medicare, Medicaid, and disability and unemployment insurance

When taxes collected are insufficient to cover expenditures, government borrows from creditors (just as individuals, households, and corporations do).

The money spent by the U.S. government goes mostly to privately produced goods and services, but a significant portion is publicly spent. Some of these expenditures are made in order to regulate various aspects of commerce; maintain a payments system and manage the nation's money supply; and provide social insurance (e.g., Social Security, Medicare, and Medicaid) in the economy, which is called "transfer payments."

INSTITUTIONAL INFRASTRUCTURE

Just as a household must spend money on necessities like mortgage (or rent), food and drink, clothing, transportation to/from work and school, child care, education, health care, etc., the government also has basic spending needs.

A critical function of the government is to develop and maintain the institutions that will allow private citizens and companies to function and prosper in the modern, global marketplace.

An important aspect of the institutional infrastructure is the definition and enforcement of property rights and contracts via a legal system consisting of federal and local courts. In addition, fire and police protection is essential. The government also has an important regulatory function. When natural monopolies (such as utility companies) emerge, regulation of the quantity and price of the goods (and/or services) produced by the monopolist may help level the playing field. Government spending on these functions is necessary, provided that a certain balance is maintained.

Encouraging innovation and competition contributes to economic growth, and there are agencies within the U.S. government that serve this function. The long list includes the Centers for Disease Control and Prevention (CDC), the Environmental Protection Agency (EPA), the Federal Communications Commission (FCC), the Federal Emergency Management Agency (FEMA), the Federal Trade Commission (FTC), the Food and Drug Administration (FDA), the Occupational Safety and Health Administration (OSHA), the Social Security Administration (SSA), the Transportation Security Administration (TSA), and others. These agencies have mandates to regulate a wide range of goods and services and provide guidance to the private sector on key consumption and production decisions.

The prospect of monopoly profits for some companies for at least some period of time (often through patent protection) provides incentives for innovation. Government does not seek to discourage this but rather tries to balance encouraging innovation and competition.

The activities and budgets of some of these agencies are not entirely free of controversy, but they are widely recognized as serving a useful purpose, and their budgets are fairly small compared with those of cabinet-level departments.

MONETARY POLICY

A critically important role played by the federal government is to maintain a stable financial system and conduct monetary policy. These functions are entrusted to the Federal Reserve System (the Fed), which acts as the central bank for the United States. Together with its twelve regional reserve banks, the Federal Reserve serves three critical functions for the U.S. economy.

First, it provides a variety of financial services to depository institutions in the country's payments systems, such as the retail service of distributing currency and coin, collecting checks, and transferring funds electronically through the automated clearinghouse. In other words, our day-to-day payment systems are facilitated by the Fed.

Second, the Federal Reserve supervises and regulates the financial system, including bank holding companies, diversified financial holding companies,[1] foreign banks with U.S. operations, and other banks.[2]

Third, and most important, the Federal Reserve conducts monetary policy under the guidance of the Federal Reserve Act. Under this act, the Fed's responsibility is to "promote the goals of maximum employment, stable prices, and moderate long-term interest rates."

The instruments available to the Fed to accomplish its short-run goals are: "open market operations" (OMOs), "reserve requirements," and directly lending to banks at the "discount rate."

OMOs are purchases and sales of U.S. Treasury bonds that impact the federal funds rate (the interest rate at which large banks lend balances to one another overnight). Purchases of Treasury bonds by the Fed increase bank reserves and result in lower interest rates, a tool used in recessions to increase liquidity in the economy.[3]

Reserve requirements are funds that must be held by a depository institution in the form of vault cash or deposits with the Federal Reserve banks against specified deposit liabilities.

The discount rate is the interest rate charged to commercial banks and other depository institutions on loans they receive from their regional Federal Reserve bank's lending facility. Lowering the discount rate during recessions allows more banks to borrow from the Fed, raising liquidity in the financial system.

In addition to the Fed's domestic monetary policy goals, its actions also influence the international price of the U.S. dollar, and therefore the Fed sometimes engages in sales and purchases of the dollar in foreign currency markets to affect the exchange rate.

---

1 These institutions were formed after the Financial Services Modernization Act of 1999, also known as the Gramm-Leach-Bliley Act, which repealed part of the Glass-Steagall Act of 1933, which prohibited any institution from acting as any combination of an investment bank, a commercial bank, and an insurance company.

2 In addition to the Fed, there are other agencies that help supervise the stability of the financial system. In particular, under the Dodd-Frank Act of 2010, the Financial Stability Oversight Council (FSOC) has been created with a statutory mandate to identify emerging risks and contain excessive risks in the financial system. The FSOC is a collaborative body that brings together the Treasury, the Fed, the Office of the Comptroller of the Currency, the Consumer Financial Protection Bureau, the Securities and Exchange Commission, the Federal Deposit Insurance Corporation, the Commodity Futures Trading Commission, the Federal Housing Finance Agency, the National Credit Union Administration, and an insurance expert appointed by the president and confirmed by the Senate for a six-year term.

3 During the recent financial crisis, the Fed also purchased mortgage-backed securities and other assets.

A great majority of economists have supported the decisions made by the Federal Reserve System over the past few years. In fact, monetary policy has probably helped prevent a second Great Depression.

CORRECTING MARKET FAILURES

Another important role of the government is to intervene in the normal operations of the marketplace if there are market failures. We will describe some of the instances in which the market may not deliver an optimal outcome. First, this discussion will require a clear understanding of what economists call "externalities" and "public goods."

EXTERNALITIES

Externalities are benefits or costs associated with the production or consumption of certain goods and services that are not included in their price. There are good externalities, such as the fact that a farmer maintaining a flower garden helps a beekeeper's honey production without the farmer being compensated for the benefit. There are also bad externalities—pollution is the best example.

Externalities underscore the difference between the "private" cost (or benefit) and "society's" cost (or benefit) of various goods and services.

Imagine that you are attending a football game. Let's assume that it is a close game and the fan directly in front of you always stands up and screams, even when the play is dead. Presumably, this fan is enjoying the game and is very happy. However, it is possible that his enjoyment is bothering you and therefore producing a negative externality that reduces your enjoyment of the game. This is what economists mean by a "negative consumption externality." You would be happier if this obnoxious fan would leave the game early!

Extending this notion of externality to a case of production, now imagine that a power plant uses coal to produce electricity. But, as a by-product, it emits dangerous gases that produce sulfuric and nitric acids. Clearly, this can damage nearby buildings and the environment. And the damage may not be restricted to nearby, as wind and rain can deliver these pollutants to areas that are hundreds of miles away.

Here, the total cost of producing electricity to society, which is the sum of the price paid by consumers and some consideration for pollution, exceeds the private cost, which is just the price paid by consumers. The consumers are not paying extra to account for the pollution their electricity use (through its production) is causing. If we were to tax the use of electricity to reflect the pollution aspect, then the higher electricity price would lead to a lower quantity of electricity used. This lower quantity of electricity would better represent the socially optimal (taking into account the pollution) amount of electricity. Therefore, in the absence of a pollution tax, the production of electricity will exceed the socially desirable amount. A negative externality means that the social cost (with the additional tax) is higher than the private cost of producing.

Should we outlaw the use of coal in the production of electricity? What should be done about the discrepancy between the social and private costs of production?

One possibility is for the government to regulate the amount of pollutants released into the atmosphere, compliance with which typically requires a firm to add equipment to its chimneys. This

13

equipment cost could otherwise be used to hire more workers or to enlarge the production capacity, and therefore it also comes at a social cost.

It may be better to use taxes to eliminate production inefficiencies. The government would impose a per-unit tax on the production of electricity equal to the difference between the social and private marginal costs of production—thus, the economically optimal quantity of electricity would be produced. In addition, the tax revenue collected might reduce other taxes that create economic inefficiencies.

However, it is difficult to accurately estimate the size of these taxes and subsidies (in the case of positive externalities). Furthermore, it may be the case that taxes imply zero production as economically efficient in certain cases. Indeed, some researchers use this argument to support the prohibition of drugs. And the so-called cap-and-trade proposals, which call for limiting emissions and then allowing producers to buy or sell "rights" to a defined volume of emissions, derive their economic rationale from a similar approach—a market is formed to trade for "pollution rights."

These are all economically reasonable solutions. In practice, however, the solution to the problem of externalities is government intervention, usually with a mandate that restricts production or sets targets for the amount of "acceptable pollution." For example, in July 2011, the federal government announced a new gas mileage target for car manufacturers of 55 miles per gallon by year 2025, a requirement many consider a public good.

PUBLIC GOODS

We can classify goods and services as public or private based on whether others can also enjoy or consume them versus whether other consumers can be excluded from the consumption process. For example, a slice of pizza is defined as a "pure private good" because consumers are rivals in consumption. If you eat a slice, then that slice is no longer available to me. Also, one can be easily excluded from consumption. If I do not pay the slice's price, I cannot consume it. A large number of goods and services fall into this category.

Certain goods and services, however, can be consumed in ways that do not exclude others. For example, my neighbor and I are not rivals in receiving the signal from a satellite service provider. The signal is sent to all my neighbors in my city. But I can be easily excluded from the consumption of entertainment services provided by the signal if I do not legally own a decoder or receiver. Consequently, satellite TV service is an "impure good," with features of both private and public goods.

On the other hand, when an individual takes the freeway to drive from his home in Los Angeles to his office, other drivers and this individual are rivals. They are certainly not racing on public streets (although at times it may seem that way), but they are clearly rivals for the space on public streets. There is no credible way to exclude a particular individual from driving on the freeway, and therefore this transportation service is neither a pure public good nor a pure private good. Thus, freeway transportation is usually classified as an impure good.

Yet other goods and services do not foster rivalry among consumers and, at the same time, do not exclude any consumer from consumption. Such goods are considered "pure public goods." The prime example is a country's national defense. If the government is providing national defense services, citizens are not rivals; if some citizens are protected, then the rest of us get the same protection.

This is different from the pizza example cited earlier—a piece of pizza is gone as soon as an individual has consumed it. Furthermore, the government cannot legally or realistically exclude citizens from consuming national defense services. Therefore, we call national defense a pure public good.

What is the importance of this distinction? Can the private sector produce public goods just like it produces private (and impure) goods?

It turns out that Adam Smith's "invisible hand" (the idea that a free market will find an optimal disbursement of resources in an economy) does not achieve the best outcome in the allocation of resources in the case of public goods. Left to its own devices, the private sector will underproduce these goods, as a result of the "free-rider problem"; because we know that we cannot be excluded from the consumption of national defense services, we have an incentive not to pay for it, as we expect that we can "free ride" and our neighbors will pick up the tab. Since everyone has this incentive to free ride, the outcome is a less than socially desirable level of national defense. In this situation, it is better for society that the government intercede to correct this market failure.

The free-rider problem can be quite significant in the delivery of radio or TV content. For example, local public radio and TV stations in the United States have many more listeners or viewers than subscribers or donators—for this reason, they hold annual subscription or donation drives. They do not have an enforcement mechanism and must instead rely on individuals' senses of responsibility to raise funds.

In the United States, a significant number of TV broadcasts are free. However, in other countries, for example Japan, the central government charges each resident a fee to finance the public TV broadcast costs. High penalty fees and periodic checks deter free riding.

EVALUATING PUBLIC GOODS

The production of pure public goods is usually undertaken by the government. Since they are not sold in private markets, it is difficult to determine the true value of public projects to society. Costs are typically measured as the cost of inputs (wages) and other materials used in the production of the public project. Surveys and "revealed preference arguments" are also used to value these projects.

Another challenge is to estimate the demand for these goods and services. Since there is no established way of doing this, the government typically responds to the most organized and vocal interest groups in determining what is produced, and in what volume. As the benefits of publicly produced goods and services tend to be concentrated on a small group of individuals, either locally focused or demographically narrowly defined, and since the costs are borne by a much larger group, if not the entire population, some of the public goods may be overproduced, or the composition of the production may be far from the socially desirable outcome. An example of this kind of inefficiency is "pork barrel" spending in the form of agricultural subsidies, public works projects, and certain defense spending projects whose benefits are concentrated in a small number of congressional districts but whose costs are spread over all American taxpayers.

17

This last point highlights the importance of political considerations in the allocation of goods and services in the economy. Given the diverse preferences over economic and social outcomes throughout an economy, how does the society organize so as to aggregate these preferences and bring about a favorable economic and social outcome?

Public choice theory takes the view that there are frictions in the political arena that prevent the government from taking actions that a benevolent government would take in the interest of its citizens. These political frictions have the potential to shape a government's economic and political agenda.

WHAT ARE PUBLIC GOODS?

We can look at the entire U.S. budget and make a strong case for the government to produce a variety of goods and services.

National defense is clearly a pure public good and therefore ought to be produced by the government. But what about education? Education is not a pure public good. Increasing the number of students in a classroom may cause a teacher's educational performance to suffer, making students rivals in the consumption of the teacher's services. Also, some individuals are often excluded—most universities, public or private, have formal student selection procedures.

However, there are also some clear benefits arising from positive externalities of education. The quality of life in a country may be higher if the citizenry is better educated. Better-informed individuals can evaluate economic and social issues more intelligently, may have a better attitude toward legal versus criminal activities, and may lead more productive lives.

The real question is how to deliver educational services. Should the government be directly involved in the production via public schools? In addition to private schools, would a voucher system enhance competition among all schools and raise the quality of education?

K–12 education can be viewed as a public good; this quantity of education produces significant positive externalities and hence government intervention seems justified to increase its production to socially optimal levels. This still leaves open the question of exactly how the production should be carried out. But leaving aside the voucher issue for the time being, can we make the same positive externality claim about college or postgraduate education? There is strong evidence that the positive externality is "internalized" by the college-educated individual, as a graduate's lifetime earnings are significantly higher than a nongraduate's. The same can be said about postgraduate education. Higher education helps both society and the individual, but, economically speaking, it should be the individual's responsibility.

SOCIAL INSURANCE

Since most individuals are risk-averse, they value insurance so that their consumptions do not fluctuate excessively even if there are changes in their personal situation. In other words, they desire to maintain a reasonable level of consumption even when they are unemployed, or sick, or retired, relative to when they were employed, healthy, or in the workforce. In a perfect world, private markets could deal with these insurance demands and provide a vehicle to smooth consumption over time as individuals' professional and personal situations change.

In practice, however, insurance against these individual risks does not exist, mainly because of asymmetric information, which means buyers and sellers of certain goods and services possess varying amounts of information.

One response to this kind of market failure is the public provision of insurance. In this case, however, there is a related problem created by the government, called "moral hazard." If an individual has access to insurance against a particular risk, let's say unemployment, then he can be very picky in his job choice and lower his search intensity. As a result, the duration of unemployment can be very long, and this creates an inefficiency. With workers' compensation insurance, it is sometimes difficult to determine whether an injury is real or faked, and if it is real, whether it happened at work or elsewhere. If the workers' compensation insurance is generous, then there is an incentive on the part of individuals to make false claims and, once again, moral hazard produced by the public provision of insurance creates an inefficiency.

In America, there is public insurance for unemployment, disability, health, and old age (retirement security). The important question is whether the private market fails to deliver efficient quantities of insurance in these cases.

Another way to put this is to ask whether the benefits of government-provided insurance outweigh the costs to society due to moral hazard and the related negative impact on employment, savings, and output.

HEALTH INSURANCE

There are two major types of health insurance. The first is private health insurance, mostly provided by employers with some deductibles, copayments, and coinsurance rates. Companies pay for most of the premiums because these reduce their tax liability. In addition, large groups of individuals allow for risk pooling, making the risks, and therefore the premiums, largely predictable.

The second major type of health insurance is publicly provided: in the U.S., Medicare for individuals 65 and older and Medicaid for low-income individuals regardless of age, along with health benefits for active military members and veterans.

These health expenditures, especially Medicare costs, have ballooned to over 20% of the federal budget, and, with the projected aging of the U.S. population, they pose a significant challenge to policy makers in the years ahead. At the same time, the exclusion of employer-sponsored health insurance from taxable income is the largest "tax spending" item. Health insurance expenditures, direct and indirect, are the most significant fiscal issue facing America.

SOCIAL SECURITY

Social Security provides a stable income during retirement as long as the individual is alive, or if a breadwinner dies and the spouse needs funds to survive. Since retirement tends to be at an age that is known in advance, self-insurance can work well to provide for old-age consumption. Given the highly predictable age of retirement, why doesn't the individual himself save during working years and take care of consumption when old? Why do we need the involvement of government at all?

The private market does offer annuity contracts that pay out a certain stream of income after retirement as long as the individual is alive, and some of these contracts have survivor benefits. However, this market is quite thin, because individuals who expect to live a long life value such contracts, and since the insurance companies anticipate this self-selection, they price the contracts in such a way as to price out nearly everyone. Enter the need for a mandatory annuity program, Social Security.

Another reason for government involvement in pensions or longevity insurance is that some policy makers believe that individuals are myopic and will not save for their retirement themselves. As a result, the government maintains an unfunded retirement system, collecting taxes from current workers and distributing the proceeds as pensions to current retirees.

Social insurance programs are by far the largest items in the government's budget. As a result, they are the primary drivers of current and future budget challenges that, if left unresolved, threaten the growth performance of the U.S. economy. In future chapters, we will highlight the budgetary implications of social insurance programs and what current academic research suggests about possible solutions.

Key points in this chapter:

- We must have a government to provide the infrastructure for the private sector to do its job properly. Maintaining the legal system, protecting property rights, maintaining prudent regulation, providing police and fire protection, and sustaining a stable financial system and sound monetary policy are good for the private citizenry. These expenditures are justified for the most part.

- In addition, the government must spend money to provide key public goods. These include defense and primary and secondary educational expenditures, a significant sharing of college education costs, and providing research institutions with R&D support.

- Finally, the government must fulfill its social insurance function, helping the members of society insure against basic risks, such as those in the areas of health, longevity, disability, and unemployment.

This still leaves two important questions unanswered:

- How much of these expenditures must the government make?

- How should these expenditures be financed?

In the next chapter, we will describe how much spending the government has historically done and on what types of items. Later, we will examine the revenue side of the government's budget and explain the effects of taxation on the economy.

Only after considering the two sides of the government's budget carefully, in both a historical and an international context, can we understand the significance of U.S. budget deficits.

CHAPTER 3
THE U.S. ECONOMY AT LARGE

In the previous chapter, we argued that there are certain expenditures that the government must make in order to place the private sector in a sound economic environment. Rather than prescribe specific dollar amounts for expenditures, we laid out the general economic principles that support the various public agencies and institutions.

In this chapter, we ask:

- How do we measure what an economy produces in a year?

- How does the economy work, and what makes it grow in the long run?

- What are the facts about government spending?

- What are the facts about the government's tax collections?

25

• How are the budget deficit and government debt related to spending and revenues?

At the end of this chapter, we list the important take-aways regarding the size of the U.S. government, its historical trends, and comparisons between it and other developed countries. In much of the discussion that follows, we present government expenditures and revenues relative to gross domestic product (GDP) or gross national product (GNP) to facilitate comparisons over time and across different countries. This chapter begins with two measures of economic activity.

MEASURING PROSPERITY

How do we measure an individual's or a nation's well-being?

The best indicators of well-being are measures of income, such as income per person or GDP per person. If we see that an individual is enjoying a larger quantity and quality of goods and services as measured by income over time, then this consumer is clearly becoming better off. Similarly, if we see a nation with an increasing GDP per person over time, we say that that nation is becoming richer. But does money buy happiness?

Of course, there are factors other than money, or income and consumption, that are important for happiness. These include good health and longevity, a clean environment, safety and security, democratic rights, and some subjective notion of economic equality. However, these aspects of life tend to be very highly correlated with measures of income and consumption. As a result, we rely on the traditional macroeconomic measurements, such as GNP or GDP, to assess economic well-being.[4]

GROSS DOMESTIC PRODUCT AND GROSS NATIONAL PRODUCT

The first macroeconomic indicator typically used to measure economic activity in a country or region is "nominal GDP," which is the market value of all final goods and services produced in an economy during a given time period.[5] This is based on the current market value of goods and services and, as such, can change as a result of changes in prices. Thus, a more useful indicator is "real GDP," which reflects changes in physical quantities, not changes in prices. Real GDP therefore measures the quantities of all newly produced final goods and services in a country over a given time period; it is adjusted for inflation.

In addition to real GDP, which measures the economic activity within a geographic location such as the United States, economists also consider GNP, which measures real economic activity taking into consideration the nationality of the ownership of the factors of production.

---

4 For example, Jones and Klenow (2009) use data across 134 countries from 1980 to 2000 and estimate the correlation between the typical income-per-person measure used by economists and a broader measure of welfare that also incorporates a preference for longevity, income equality, and leisure. In particular, the authors ask an individual which country he would like to live in, in year 2000, without any knowledge of whether or not he will be rich or poor, how many hours of hard work he will have to endure or how many leisure hours he will enjoy, how long he may live, or whether he may even have a very short lifespan due to some serious illness. The main finding is that there is a 95% correlation between ranking countries on the basis of their income per person and using this alternative measure of welfare that incorporates concerns about health, equality, and a preference about leisure.

5 Economists distinguish between final goods and intermediate goods. Final goods are produced and consumed, while intermediate goods are used as inputs to produce a final good. For example, flour is a final good when sold directly to consumers in a supermarket but an intermediate good when sold to firms that then use the flour they purchased to make cookies. Intermediate goods are not included in GDP to avoid double counting, i.e., counting first as an intermediate good and then again as part of the final product.

For the United States, these two measures of economic activity are nearly the same: GNP exceeded GDP by about 1.3% in 2010. Therefore, the use of real GDP or real GNP will not make any difference. We will measure the living standards, income, output, or well-being of individuals with either metric.

THE RELATIONSHIP BETWEEN FACTORS OF PRODUCTION AND OUTPUT

The amount of output produced in a country depends fundamentally on its workforce, its stock of capital (such as buildings, factories, equipment, software, etc.), and the efficiency with which these factors of production are combined.

More specifically, a nation's GDP depends on the quantity of its inputs and the efficiency with which they are turned into output. Capital and labor are the two most important inputs for the production of goods and services. The overall efficiency with which capital and labor are used to produce output is referred to as "total factor productivity" (TFP).

Policies that alter incentives to work or incentives to accumulate capital have a direct impact on GDP and total income in a country. In addition, economic institutions and policies that foster innovation and technological improvements increase total factor productivity. Thus, it is important to understand the relationship between the inputs and output, as measured by GDP.

Economists summarize the relationship between these factors of production and output with a mathematical expression, commonly referred to as a "Cobb-Douglas production function."[6] This function can be used, as we will show in the next section, to more closely examine the factors that drive changes in output by isolating the effects of changes in labor, capital, and productivity.

Using this function, we can understand how government policies that impact labor and capital will alter the path of GDP in a country over time.

GROWTH OF REAL GROSS DOMESTIC PRODUCT IN THE U.S., 1870–2008

The prosperity of America between 1870 and 2008, as measured by real GDP, is displayed in *Figure 3.1*.

Two key features demonstrated in this figure are that real income increases over time, and that there are some short-term fluctuations around this positive trend. For example, there is a 30% decline in real GDP below its long-run trend during the Great Depression of 1929 to 1933.

---

6 The mathematical formula for this Cobb-Douglas production: $Y_t = A_t K_t^{0.4} L_t^{0.6}$

Here, Y_t represents real GDP, A_t represents TFP, K_t represents the capital input (measured as the real value of private fixed assets and the stock of consumer durables), and L_t represents the labor input (measured as total hours of work), all at time period T. In this formula, the exponents of 0.4 and 0.6 are referred to as the "output elasticities" of capital and labor, respectively. These elasticities measure the sensitivity of output to changes in these two inputs. More precisely, these elasticities measure the percentage change in output, Y_t, due to a 1% change in capital, K_t, or labor, L_t. Alternatively, these exponents reflect shares of capital and labor in national income.

29

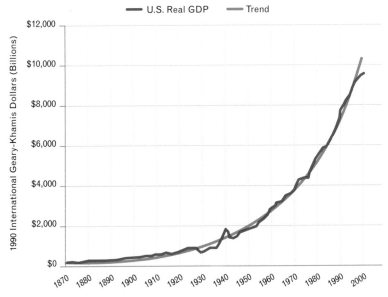

Source: Maddison (2010), Table 2, GDP levels 1 AD-2008 AD.
Note: 1 thousand billion equals 1 trillion.

Figure 3.1: Real GDP in the U.S, 1870–2008

Growth in real GDP during World War II is also apparent. Real GDP peaked at $1.7136 trillion in 1944, more than doubling from its 1929 level in just 16 years. The average annual growth rate of real U.S. GDP between 1870 and 2008 was about 3%. The rate of growth in real GDP was higher in the second half of the 20th century (3.5%) than in the first half (3.0%). However, since 2000, real GDP has grown less than 3% per year, with the exception of 2004 and 2005.

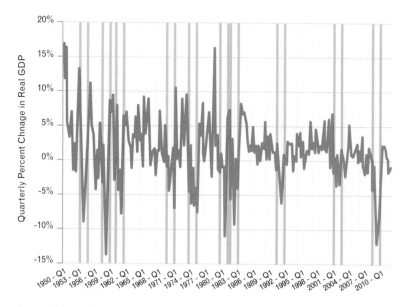

Source: Bureau of Economic Analysis (2011). NIPA Table 1.1, last revised on August 26, 2011.

Figure 3.2. Growth Rates of Real GDP in the U.S., 1950:Q1–2011:Q2

More recent economic fluctuations can be observed better in *Figure 3.2*, which displays the growth rate of real GDP between the first quarter of 1950 and the second quarter of 2011.

In this figure, gray bars indicate the beginning and ending dates of U.S. recessions as determined by the National Bureau of Economic Research (NBER).[7] The December 2007–June 2009 recession, with an 8.9% decline in real GDP in the last quarter of 2008, represented one of the largest contractions of the U.S. economy since the 1950s.

---

7 NBER is a "private, nonprofit, nonpartisan research organization" (www.nber.org/info. html) dedicated to studying the science and empirics of economics.

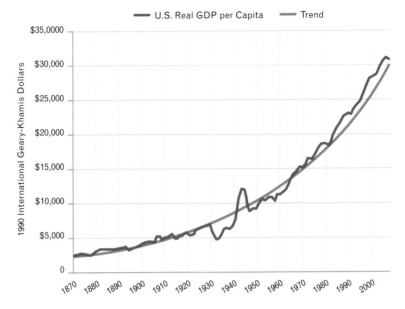

Source: Maddison (2010), Table 3, per capita GDP levels 1 AD–2008 AD.

Figure 3.3. Real GDP per Person in the U.S., 1870–2008

While these charts allow us to examine the changes in the overall economy, it is also important to consider the changes in GDP per person, which takes into account changes in population. *Figure 3.3* displays real GDP per capita in the U.S. over the same time period as *Figure 3.1*. The average annual growth rate of real GDP per person over this time period has been about 2%. There has been a 12-fold increase in real GDP per person since 1870 and a threefold increase between 1950 and 2008.

How was this tremendous increase in living standards achieved? What were the sources of economic growth? Have other countries had similar experiences?

WHAT IS THE ENGINE OF ECONOMIC GROWTH?

Economic growth raises our living standards. What drives growth? If we understand where economic growth comes from, then we can better design institutions and policies to create it.[8]

Real GNP

	Real GNP	Per Capita	Labor	Capital	TFP
1960-2009	3.14	1.68	1.50	2.96	1.03
1960-1973	4.28	2.48	2.38	3.87	1.27
1973-1995	2.82	1.43	1.60	2.46	0.86
1995-2009	2.58	1.33	0.53	2.91	1.09

Source: Authors' calculations.

Table 3.1. Growth Accounting for the U.S., 1960–2009

Table 3.1 displays growth accounting data for the U.S. between 1960 and 2009. Over this period, real GNP and real GNP per person grew at 3.14% and 1.68% per year, respectively. The growth rates of labor and capital inputs during that period were 1.5% and 2.96%, respectively. Consequently, contributions of labor, capital, and TFP to the 3.14% growth in real GNP were all about 1 percentage point (Note: We use the growth accounting equation $\%\Delta Y = \%\Delta A + 0.4\%\Delta K + 0.6\%\Delta L$, which yields $3.14\% = 1.03\% + 0.6 \times 1.50\% + 0.4 \times 2.96\%$).

---

8 We use the Cobb-Douglas production function to obtain the growth accounting equation: $\%\Delta Y = \%\Delta A + 0.4\%\Delta K + 0.6\%\Delta L$.

According to this equation, growth in real GNP ($\%\Delta Y$) comes from three sources: growth in total factor productivity ($\%\Delta A$); growth in capital input ($\%\Delta K$), multiplied by the share of capital in national income (0.4); and growth in labor input ($\%\Delta L$), again appropriately scaled (0.6).

However, there are substantial differences in the growth rates and the contributions of different factors to growth across different periods. For example, the period between 1973 and 1995 is known as the period of productivity slowdown when the TFP growth rate declined to 0.86%. Another striking difference is the decline in the growth rate of labor in the 1995–2009 period, which is mostly due to the recession in 2008 and 2009.

To summarize, long-run economic growth comes from healthy growth in labor, capital, and TFP. What kind of policies and institutions foster growth in the factors of production and productivity? What is the role of the government in designing an economic environment that leads to prosperity? Before we tackle these questions, it is useful to examine the experiences of other developed countries in terms of long-run economic growth.

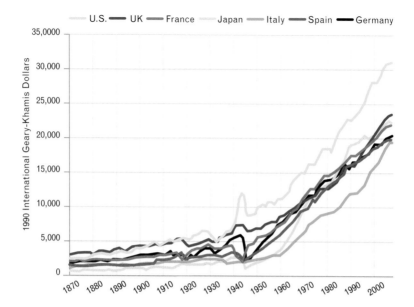

Source: Maddison (2010), Table 3, per capita GDP levels 1 AD–2008 AD.

Figure 3.4. Real GDP per Capita by Country, 1870–2008

LEARNING FROM OTHER COUNTRIES

Figure 3.4 displays real GDP per capita for the United States, the United Kingdom, France, Germany, Japan, Italy, and Spain between 1870 and 2008.[9] All the countries in this group have demonstrated significant growth rates over this time period. Thus, the high-growth experience is not unique to the United States.

---

9 Data are from Maddison (2010), where a purchasing power parity (PPP) exchange rate is used to compare baskets of goods across countries instead of relying on nominal exchange rates, which may not accurately reflect the price of goods that are consumed in each country.

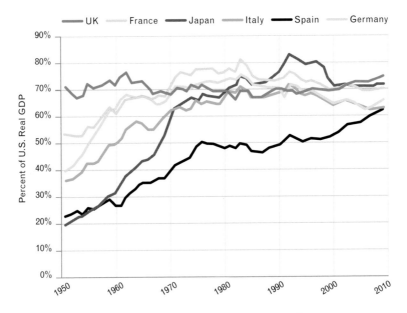

Source: Maddison (2010), Table 3, per capita GDP levels 1 AD–2008 AD.

Figure 3.5. Real GDP per Capita Relative to the U.S.

Figure 3.5 displays real GDP per capita in the United Kingdom, France, Germany, Japan, Italy, and Spain relative to (as a fraction of) real GDP per capita in the U.S. from 1950 to 2008. Real GDP per capita in the United Kingdom in 1950 was about 70% of the U.S. level. Almost 60 years later, this ratio was still below 80%.

Japan and Spain demonstrate significant catch-up over this period. In 1950, GDP per capita in these two countries was about 20% of U.S. GDP per capita. By 2008, Japan and Spain had reached more than 70% and 60% of the U.S. level, respectively. Japan's GDP per person rose from 20% of the U.S. level in 1950 to 85% by 1991, surpassing all five other countries. However, since around the mid-1970s, all the countries but Spain have been hovering around 70% of U.S. real GDP per capita.

There are three noteworthy trends reflected in *Figure 3.5*. First, there is a significant disparity in income across these countries in the 1950s, ranging from 20% to 70% of the U.S. level. Second, by 2008, there is significant catch-up, when most of the countries reach levels of GDP per capita that are 60% to 75% of the U.S level. Third, for most of the countries in this sample, most of the catch-up takes place before the 1980s. This process stalls in the later period, and by 2008 there is a gap of 20% to 30% across these countries remains.

Why has the United States consistently achieved output that is 20% to 30% higher than that for other advanced economies on a per capita basis, especially over the past few decades? What economic policies have driven this growth? We will discuss some of the reasons for these gaps in the chapters that follow.

CHAPTER 4

BUDGET DEFICITS AND GOVERNMENT DEBT

The entire U.S. government (federal, state, and local combined) spent more than $5.6 trillion in 2011.

This is a large number.

It is nearly 40% of the U.S. GDP. It is as large as the entire GDP of Japan, and it is just a shade below the entire GDP of China.

It is also much larger than the tax revenues of the entire U.S. government in 2011.

Why is spending so high? Where do our tax dollars go? How has spending increased so much over the past few decades?

The federal government's debt reached nearly 70% of GDP at the beginning of 2012. Compared with other countries and our own historical experience, this is not alarming in itself. However, the government incurs a "budget deficit" if it spends more than it earns through tax receipts. And these deficits must be financed through additional borrowing, which increases the national debt. With very large deficits projected for the future and with no signs of fiscal reform, the U.S. debt-to-GDP ratio will rise rapidly to alarming levels. If, for example, interest payments on government debt become as large as is projected by the Congressional Budget Office (CBO), there will have to be significant cuts to public schools, law enforcement, infrastructure, and other important expenditures.

To understand how to fix the problem, we must first examine how the U.S. government spends its money and how it generates revenues. Further, we must assess these issues relative to our own past experience and that of other countries.

OVERALL GOVERNMENT BUDGET

When a household spends more than its income, there is a deficit that must be covered by borrowing. Similarly, when the government spends more than its tax revenues, it has a budget deficit and must borrow.[10] Each year, this new borrowing adds to the existing stock of government debt. The only way to reduce the U.S. federal government's debt is to run budget surpluses. This is exactly what a household must do to reduce debt: spend less than it earns.

Until the 1970s, the U.S. federal government's budget deficits were small and infrequent, as *Figure 4.1* shows. Starting in the 1970s, deficits accumulated. Deficit reductions during the 1990s followed, and in 2000 we experienced a budget surplus of 2.4% of GDP. Since then, government outlays have again exceeded revenues, resulting in increasing deficits. The annual deficit climbed to 10% of GDP in 2009 before declining modestly in the next two years (to 8.9% in 2010 and 8.7% in 2011).

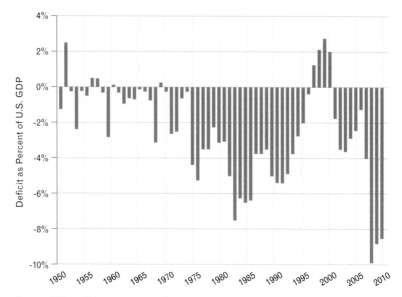

Source: Office of Management and Budget (2012), Table 1.2.

Figure 4.1. U.S. Deficits as a Percentage of GDP, 1950–2011

To finance this budget deficit, the U.S. Treasury sells bonds to the public, which increases the government debt—this can be measured in terms of public debt or gross debt (as a percentage of GDP).[11] *Figure 4.2* shows these two debt ratios from 1940 through 2011. Both public and gross debt ratios increased during

---

10 The most common notion of government budget balance is the difference between total receipts and total spending (including government consumption and investment expenditures, transfer payments, and interest payments on existing government debt). A related notion is "primary balance," which does not include the interest payments on the expenditure side.

11 Publicly held debt comprises debt held by individuals, banks, pension funds, and foreign entities, including foreign central banks. This notion of debt is typically considered net debt, as it excludes holdings of debt by other government entities. When the latter are added to public debt, we arrive at gross government debt, which includes debt held by other U.S. government entities, such as the Social Security Administration.

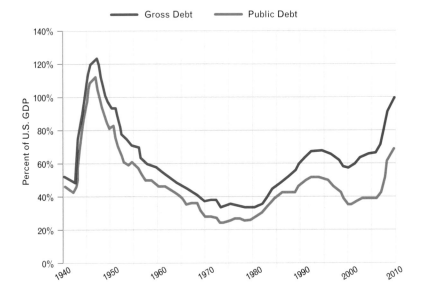

Source: Office of Management and Budget (2012), Table 7.1.

Figure 4.2. U.S. Debt as a Percentage of GDP, 1940–2011

World War II and then steadily declined through 1980. The national debt began increasing again (as a percentage of GDP) from 30% to about 40% following tax cuts during the Reagan administration (1981–1989).

Following the Great Recession of 2007–2009, there has been a precipitous jump in the public debt ratio, reaching 68% in 2011. Similarly, the gross federal government debt-to-GDP ratio increased from 69% in 2008 to 94% in 2011, the highest it has been since World War II. The debt ratio is projected to climb even further, approaching 100%, unless federal spending is cut and/or taxes are increased.[12]

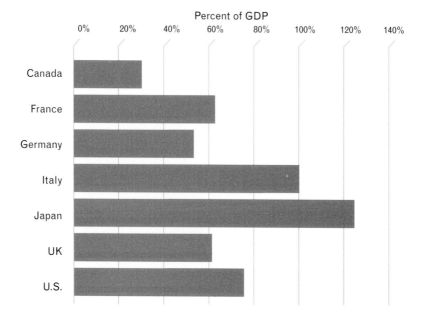

Source: OECD (2012). Economic Outlook 90 database, Annex Table 33.

Figure 4.3. Net Debt as a Percentage of GDP, 2011

Such ballooning debt raises numerous concerns about its effect on future generations. A growing debt could result in higher future interest rates and an increasing share of GDP being spent on servicing these interest payments. With higher interest rates in the future, buying homes and obtaining student loans will be much harder. They will also result in a higher cost of capital for businesses, which will impede investment and job creation.

Growing debt also raises the specter of inflation and the question of whether government budgets can be sustained in the future. On this score, it is instructive to compare our debt position

12 In addition to the debt accumulated by the federal government, states in the U.S. have been running significant deficits in recent years. Total state and local government debt in 2011 is estimated to be $2.8627 trillion, or 26% of GDP.

with that of other developed nations. *Figure 4.3* compares the net debt[13] (as percentage of GDP) ratios of the U.S. and several other developed nations in 2011.

As the figure shows, France, Germany, and the United Kingdom's net debt was around or less than 60% of their GDP, whereas ours was more than 70%.

Two countries, Italy and Japan, had higher net-debt ratios compared with ours in 2011, and both have faced negative consequences. Italy's net-debt ratio has hovered around 100% for several years, and its borrowing cost has increased in recent years as investors have begun to demand a significant risk premium to hold the government's euro-denominated debt. Japan has pursued massive government spending programs over the past two decades in an attempt to spur its anemic economy, but it has ended up with only a very large public debt to pay, without much to show in the form of economic growth.

The populations of these developed countries are aging rapidly. As a result, these countries can expect to bear higher transfer payments (related to retirement benefits and medical expenses) in the future, which could increase their debt ratios dramatically. Thus, policy makers in these developed nations are searching for ways to avoid default on their national debt. In the U.S., we face a similar challenge in the near future as our baby boomers retire in growing numbers.

GOVERNMENT SPENDING

How much does the U.S. government spend? Where do our tax dollars go? Why has spending increased so much over the past few decades?

CATEGORIES OF GOVERNMENT SPENDING

Government spending falls into four categories:

- Purchases of goods and services

- Transfer payments

- Interest payments on existing debt

- Subsidies (e.g., price support payments to farmers)

Total government spending (at the federal, state, and local levels combined) in all these categories amounted to 37.3% of GDP (or about $5.6 trillion) in 2011.[14] The lion's share of this spending (about $5.4 trillion) is related to only the first two categories: purchases and transfer payments.[15]

Government purchases consist of "consumption expenses" and "investment expenditures." Government consumption expenses accounted for $2.5 trillion, or 16.9% of GDP, in 2011.[16] Such

---

13 The Organisation for Economic Co-operation and Development (OECD) definition of net debt is "the gross financial liabilities of the general government sector less the financial assets of the general government sector. Such assets may be cash, bank deposits, loans to the private sector, participation in private sector companies, holdings in public corporations, or foreign exchange reserves, depending on the institutional structure of the country concerned and data availability."

14 Our definition of total government spending corresponds to current expenditures plus gross government investment in the National Income and Product Accounts (NIPA).

15 The remaining two categories of government spending (interest payments or subsidies) are relatively minor. Interest payments on government debt ($428.3 billion) and subsidies ($62.7 billion) comprised relatively small shares of GDP in 2011, at 2.8% and 0.4%, respectively.

16 The remainder of government purchases was due to government investment expenditures of $483.3 billion, or 3.2% of U.S. GDP, in 2011.

expenses include government spending on national defense; public order and safety (police, fire, law courts, and prisons); general public services such as executive and legislative activities, tax collection, and financial management; economic affairs; health; recreation and culture; education; and income security. Government investment expenditures include spending on roads, buildings, bridges, and other infrastructure needs.

Transfer payments constituted $2.4 trillion, or 15.7% of GDP, in 2011. This expense (related to government payments to individuals in return for which the government does not receive any goods or services) includes Social Security, welfare, and disability payments; medical benefits such as expenditures on Medicare and Medicaid; income maintenance benefits; unemployment compensation; veterans' benefits; and education and training assistance.

To give you an idea of the government's overall spending in all four categories above, *Table 4.1* breaks out total government spending in 2011 into spending by the federal government, and by state and local governments.

The federal government's largest expenditure item was transfer payments, followed by consumption expenses. Transfer payments were about $1.8 trillion in 2011, accounting for 46.2% of the federal government's spending that year.

	Federal Government		State and Local Government	
	Billions of Dollars	Percentage of Total Spending	Billions of Dollars	Percentage of Total Spending
Consumption Expenditure	1,072.0	27.3	1,475.2	64.9
Gross Government Investment	160.8	4.1	322.5	14.2
Current Transfer Payments	1,813.3	46.2	558.0	24.5
Grants-in-aid to State and Local Government	492.5	12.5	–	–
Subsidies	62.3	1.6	0.5	–
Interest Payments	312.4	8.0	116.0	5.1
Capital Transfer Payments	80.0	2.0	–	–
Investment Grants to State and Local Governments	71.4	1.8	–	–
Other	(138.0)	(3.5)	(198.7)	(8.7)
Total Spending	**3,926.8**	**100.0**	**2,273.4**	**100.0**

Source: Bureau of Economic Analysis (2012). Tables 3.1, 3.2, 3.3, last revised February 29, 2012. Note: Total government spending excludes transfer payments from federal to state and local governments. In 2011, these transfers totaled $492.5 billion in grants-in-aid and $71.4 billion in investment grants.

Table 4.1. U.S. Federal vs. State Government Spending, 2011

Consumption expenditures were about $1.07 trillion in 2011, constituting 27.3% of the federal government's spending. State and local governments' largest spending category was consumption (64.9%), which includes spending on K–12 and higher education, health and human services, transportation services, corrections and rehabilitation services, and general government expenses.

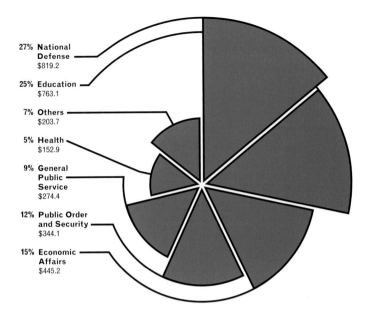

27% **National Defense** $819.2

25% **Education** $763.1

7% **Others** $203.7

5% **Health** $152.9

9% **General Public Service** $274.4

12% **Public Order and Security** $344.1

15% **Economic Affairs** $445.2

Source: Bureau of Economic Analysis (2011). NIPA Table 3.15.5, last revised September 14, 2011. Note: 1. Others include income security, housing and community services, and recreation and culture. 2. Education includes elementary, secondary, and higher education, as well as libraries; economic affairs includes transportation, space and other economic affairs; public order and safety includes police, fire, law courts, and prisons; general public service includes executive and legislative services, tax collection, and financial management.

Figure 4.4 U.S. Government Purchases by Function (in $ billions), 2010

Since government expenditures are primarily due to government purchases (consumption and investments), it's worth examining these purchases in greater detail. *Figure 4.4* shows that more than half of government purchases are related to education (25%) and national defense (27%) combined.

National security expenditures (national defense as well as public order and safety expenditures) accounted for about 8% of GDP in 2010, which ranks us as the largest spender in this category (as a percentage of GDP) among developed nations. As we look for ways to trim the budget deficit, such defense-related expenses are natural targets.

TRENDS IN TOTAL
U.S. GOVERNMENT SPENDING

Government spending had increased from approximately 20.8% of GDP in 1950 to 37.3% by 2010. However, this increase has not been a gradual one. Indeed, total government expenditures fell from 34.1% of GDP in 1990 to 30.4% in 2000. After remaining at around 32% until 2007, government spending escalated rapidly (which reflects an increase of $806 billion, using the 2011 GDP figure of $15.094 trillion).

What explains this 7% increase in government spending, from 30% to 37.3% between 2000 and 2011? As we discuss further below, this increase is primarily due to a significant increase in transfer payments and the recent escalation of spending on national security, both of which have been modestly offset by lower net interest payments.

Figure 4.5 displays the long-term trends in total government expenditures and their components as a percentage of U.S. GDP.

As this figure shows, transfer payments have nearly tripled in size relative to GDP in 60 years, increasing from about 6% in 1950 to around 17.5% by 2011. Specifically, Social Security payments, which averaged 4.2% between 1984 and 2008, have increased in recent years to about 4.8% of GDP in 2009 and 2010. Medicare and Medicaid have also increased since their establishment in 1965, amounting to 3.6% and 2.8% of GDP, respectively, in 2010. The U.S. government's spending on these three programs combined accounted for 11.1% of GDP in 2010. These transfer payments are expected to rise as our baby boomers continue to retire. In fact, by 2050, the number of Americans age 65 and older is projected to be 88.5 million, which would be more than double the size of this sector in 2011.

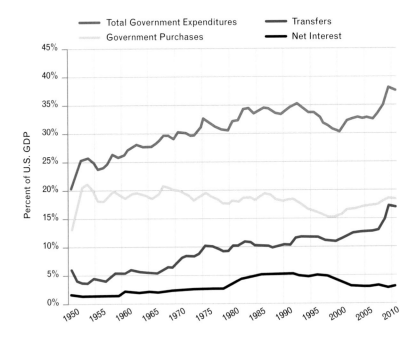

Source: Bureau of Economic Analysis (2012). NIPA Tables 1.1.5 and 3.1, last revised March 29, 2012.

Figure 4.5. Components of U.S. Government Expenditures as a Percentage of GDP, 1950–2011

Government purchases, the largest component of total government spending, averaged about 19% until the mid-1970s and declined thereafter, fluctuating around 18% until 1993. As *Figure 4.5* shows, government purchases declined further during the Clinton administration, to about 15% of GDP in 1998. However, since 2000, government purchases have been increasing, and they constituted 18.4% of GDP in 2011—an increase of more than 3 percentage points in 10 years.[17]

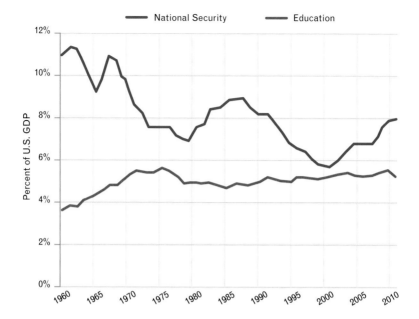

National Security — Education

Source: Bureau of Economic Analysis (2012). NIPA Table 3.15.5, last revised September 14, 2011, and Table 1.1.5, last revised March 29, 2012.

Figure 4.6. U.S. National Security and Education Expenditures as a Percentage of GDP, 1960–2010

The two largest components of government purchases are national security and education. *Figure 4.6* takes a closer look at the long-term changes in these two areas of government spending between 1960 and 2010.

- National security expenses trended downward from 1960 to about 5.8% of GDP in 2000, with an interim period in the 1980s during which such expenses increased as a percentage of GDP. National security expenses as a percentage of GDP

17 Figure 4.5 also shows that net interest payments, a small government expense category, increased in the 1980s due to greater debt balances and higher interest rates over that period.

51

declined quite significantly in the 1990s. However, following the 9/11 tragedy, government spending on national security increased to 6.8% of GDP by 2004 and remained at that level until 2007. By 2009 and 2010, government spending on national security was 8% of GDP, highest among developed nations.

• In contrast, government spending on education increased after 1960, peaking in 1975 at 5.7% of GDP, as illustrated in *Figure 4.6*. After 1975, spending on education declined to 4.7% of GDP in 1984. Since 1984, government spending on education has been increasing and averaged 4.9% of GDP in the 1980s, 5.1% in the 1990s, and 5.3% in the 2000s, peaking at 5.6% in 2009. Most recently, in the aftermath of the recent recession, government spending on education declined by 1.5% and 1.7% in 2009 and 2010, respectively.

TRENDS IN U.S. FEDERAL GOVERNMENT SPENDING

At the federal level, government spending (including federal transfers to state and local governments) has also increased significantly in recent years, from about 21% of GDP from 1960 through 2007 to 27% of GDP in 2010 (the highest since 1960). Federal government spending was about 26% of GDP in 2011— see *Figure 4.7*.[18] Federal transfers to state and local governments also increased, from 1.2% of GDP in 1960 to 3.7% in 2011.

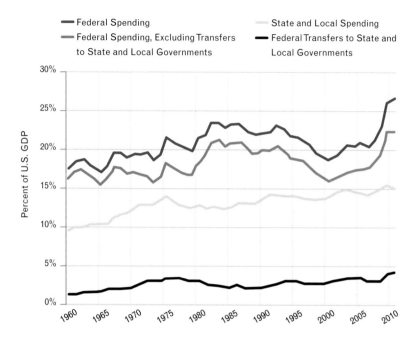

Legend:
— Federal Spending
— Federal Spending, Excluding Transfers to State and Local Governments
State and Local Spending
— Federal Transfers to State and Local Governments

Source: Bureau of Economic Analysis (2012). NIPA Tables 1.1.5 and 3.1, last revised March 29, 2012.

Figure 4.7. Total Federal Spending as a Percentage of GDP, 1960–2011

For federal government spending to return to its historical level of 21% of GDP, it should have declined by $754 billion in 2011.[19] Furthermore, to maintain the federal budget at its historical average of 21% of GDP, this reduction in federal government spending would have to be permanent. However, this spending cut might not even be sufficient to restore fiscal balance, especially in light of the projected increases in Social Security and Medicare spending.

18 There is a significant amount of transfers that flow from the federal government to state and local governments. Figure 4.7 shows total federal spending both with and without these transfers.

19 Based on 2011 GDP of $15.094 trillion.

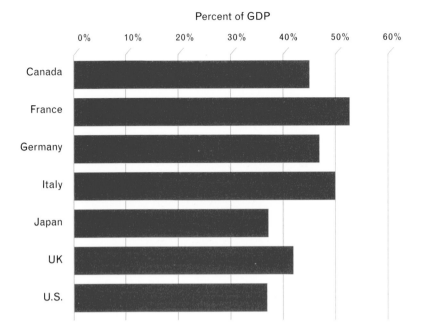

Source: OECD (2011a, 2011b). Datasets 1 and 11, extracted on April 8, 2011.

Figure 4.8. Government Expenditures as a Percentage of GDP, 1990–2008
average

LEARNING FROM OTHER COUNTRIES

Does the U.S. government spend a larger fraction of its GDP than other wealthy nations? The answer is no.

Figure 4.8 presents average total government expenditures as a percentage of GDP between 1990 and 2008 for seven countries (Canada, France, Germany, Italy, Japan, the United Kingdom, and the United States).[20] The U.S. spends the least in terms of levels of government spending relative to GDP (only Japan has had levels near the U.S.).[21] The average ratio of total government expenditures to GDP in this time period was about 50% for France, Germany, and Italy, and 36% for the United States.

If the U.S. government were to spend a fraction of its GDP similar to those of France, Germany, and Italy, without increasing its deficit, it would have to increase its tax receipts every year to the tune of 14% of its GDP—more than $2.1 trillion (given GDP of $15.094 trillion in 2011). A tax increase of this size every year would have a disastrous effect on the U.S. economy. Employment and capital would decline significantly and permanently.

Is the composition of U.S. total government expenditures different from that of other rich nations? The largest components of U.S. government purchases are expenditures on national security (defense plus public safety) and education. The next two figures provide a comparison of these components for a group of countries between 1990 and 2008.

20 Averages exclude the following time periods for which data were not available for these countries: Canada, 2007 and 2008; France, 1990–1994; and Germany, 1990.

21 Government expenditures here are defined as the sum of central (or federal) and local (state and city) expenditures. The division between expenditures by the federal government and those of state and local governments varies considerably across the OECD countries. In 2009, federal government spending constituted 90% of total spending in New Zealand but 15% in Switzerland. On average, however, 46% of total government expenditures were undertaken by the federal government across the OECD (2011a).

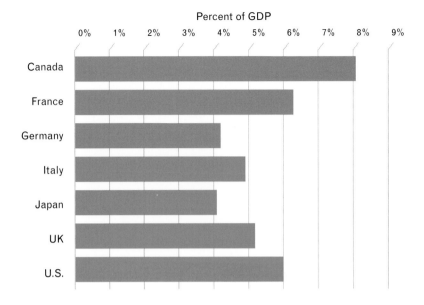

Percent of GDP

Source: OECD (2011a, 2011b). Datasets 1 and 11, extracted on April 8, 2011.

Figure 4.9. Education Expenditures as a Percentage of GDP,
1990–2008 Average

According to *Figure 4.9*, the United States is in the middle of the pack at about 6% of GDP spent on education by the government. Four countries (Japan, Germany, Italy, and the United Kingdom) spent less, on average, over this 20-year period than the United States.[22] Only Canada and France spent more on education relative to GDP than the United States.

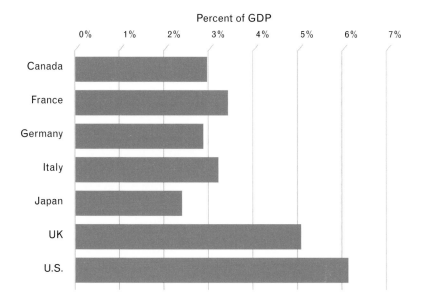

Percent of GDP

Source: OECD (2011a, 2011b). Datasets 1 and 11, extracted on April 8, 2011.

Figure 4.10. Military Spending as a Percentage of GDP,
1990–2008 Average

In military spending, the United States leads the developed nations, as *Figure 4.10* indicates.

In fact, military spending was about twice as high in the U.S. as in each of the rest of the European countries, excluding the United Kingdom, represented above from 1990 through 2008.

22 Averages exclude the following time periods for which data were not available for these countries: Canada, 2007 and 2008; France, 1990–1994; and Germany, 1990.

THE FISCAL CLIFF

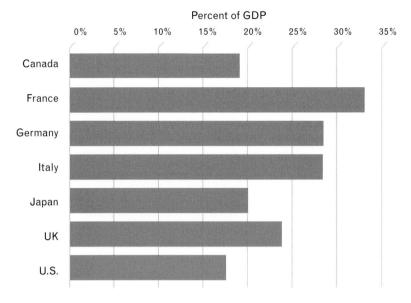

Percent of GDP

Source: OECD (2011c). Table fc-e2007, Social Expenditures Database, 2007.

Figure 4.11. Social Benefits as a Percentage of GDP, 2007

As noted earlier, another major component of government spending in the U.S. is transfer payments, including such social expenditures as retirement programs, public health spending, unemployment insurance benefits, and welfare.

Figure 4.11 shows a comparison of social expenditures as a fraction of GDP in 2007 across a set of countries.[23]

U.S. government spending in this category was 17.4% in 2007, which lagged behind all other countries shown, including Canada (the next lowest spender in this category at 18.9%) and France (the highest spender in this category at 32.8%).

Historically, gross public social expenditure has increased in many countries. In 2001, the OECD average was 22.3% of GDP.

In 2007, the OECD average had increased to 24.3% of GDP.

Social expenditures are the most significant category of government outlays for a large number of countries. With the projected aging in both the United States and European countries, these payments will significantly rise relative to national incomes. Therefore, public debate in all the developed countries is now focused on social security and medical expenditures. In the U.S., just the health care expenditures alone are projected to be almost 20% of GDP in 2080. That is more than what was spent on all government purchases in 2011, including those for national defense and education.

The rest matters less; social security and, especially, medical expenditures are the ticking financial time bomb.

23 Data on gross public social expenditures include categories such as "cash benefits (e.g., pensions, income support during maternity leave, and social assistance payments), social services (e.g., child care, care for the elderly and disabled), and tax breaks with a social purpose (e.g., tax expenditures toward families with children, or favorable tax treatment of contributions to private health plans)." This data may not be directly comparable to the NIPA data.

CHAPTER 5

GOVERNMENT RECEIPTS (TAXES)

The money going out matters, but so does the money coming in. Right now, and in the foreseeable future, the U.S. government will be spending exorbitantly more than it brings in.

TAX EXPENDITURES

Before we discuss money coming in, namely, government receipts, we must talk about money not coming in. These are the tax expenditures; money that the government does NOT collect as tax revenue because certain items are exempt from taxation or they are allowed to be deducted from taxable income.

According to the Office of Management and Budget (2012), "tax expenditures are defined in the law as 'revenue losses attributable to provisions of the federal tax laws which allow a special exclusion, exemption, or deduction from gross income or which provide a special credit, a preferential rate of tax, or a deferral of tax liability.' These exceptions may be viewed as alternatives to other policy instruments, such as spending or regulatory programs." Tax expenditures are essentially additional spending items that are hidden from the "money coming in and going out."

What are these tax expenditures, and how large are they?

The largest two are: exclusion of employer contributions for medical insurance premiums and medical care; and deductibility of mortgage interest on owner-occupied homes. In fiscal 2012, these are estimated to be $171 billion and $87 billion, respectively.

All told, there are more than 173 such tax expenditures in our tax code, for about $1.092 trillion in fiscal 2012.

This money *not* collected is about 40% of the money that *is* collected as total federal tax revenues.

A large fraction of these tax expenditures have no economic rationale. If eliminated, our tax base would increase significantly, and this would also allow the government to reduce marginal tax rates to provide incentives for job creation and growth.

SOURCES OF GOVERNMENT RECEIPTS

The largest source of money coming in for total government (federal, state, and local combined) is taxes on labor income, which is the sum of personal income taxes (33.6% of total U.S. government receipts in 2011) and payroll taxes for old age, survivors, disability, and health insurance (known as OASDHI), contributing 22.3% of revenues in 2011. The second largest source of government revenue is taxes on production and imports (mostly sales tax), constituting 26.3% of U.S. government revenues, while corporate taxes accounted for 9.3%.

In 2011, total receipts of the U.S. government were 27.6% of the U.S. GDP, as shown in *Table 5.1*. Together, the four sources of tax revenue mentioned above (personal income, payroll, production and import, and corporate) accounted for over 91% of total receipts and 25% of U.S. GDP in 2011.

	Billions of Dollars	Percentage of Total Receipts	Percentage of GDP
Personal Current Taxes	1,400.3	33.6	9.3
Taxes on Production and imports	1097.9	26.3	7.3
Taxes on Corporate Income	389.7	9.3	2.6
Contributions for Social Insurance	930.9	22.3	6.2
Current Transfer Receipts	197.0	4.7	1.3
Capital Transfer Receipts	9.8	0.2	0.1
Other	145.5	3.5	1.0
Total receipts	**4,171.1**	**100.0**	**27.8**

Source: Bureau of Economic Analysis (2012). NIPA Tables 3.1 and 1.1.5, last updated March 29, 20112. Note: Total government receipts exclude transfers received by state and local governments from the federal government. In 2011, these amounted to $492.5 billion in grants-in-aid and $71.4 billion in investment grants received by state and local governments from the federal government.

Table 5.1. Total U.S. Government Receipts, 2011

Federal, state, and local governments rely on different sources for their tax revenues. The breakout of government revenues by level is shown in *Table 5.2*.

Of total government receipts 61.7% were collected at the federal level, and 38.3% were collected at the state and local level.

Personal income and payroll taxes (imposed on wages and salaries) make up nearly 80% of the federal government's tax revenues.

The major source of income for state and local governments was tax revenue from production and imports, which includes sales and property taxes and accounted for 45.7% of total revenues. Federal current grants-in-aid and capital investment grants accounted for 26.1% of state and local government revenues, as shown in *Table 5.2* (22.8% as federal grants-in-aid, plus 3.3% of investment grants).

	Federal Government		State and Local Government		Total Government
	Billions of Dollars	Percentage of Total Receipts	Billions of Dollars	Percentage of Total Receipts	Billions of Dollars
Personal Current Taxes	1,074.7	41.7	325.7	15.1	1,400.4
Taxes on Production and imports	110.8	4.3	987.1	45.7	1,097.9
Taxes on Corporate Income	338.2	13.1	51.5	2.4	389.7
Contributions for Social Insurance	909.3	35.3	21.6	1.0	930.9
Current Transfer Receipts	67.4	2.6	129.6	6.0	197.0
Federal Grants-in-Aid	-	-	492.5	22.8	n/a
Capital Transfer Receipts	5.1	0.2	4.7	0.2	9.8
Investment Grants from Federal Government	-	-	71.4	3.3	n/a
Other	69.2	2.7	76.2	3.5	145.4
Total Receipts	**2,574.6**	**100.0**	**2,160.3**	**100.0**	
Total Receipts, excluding federal transfers	**2,574.6**	**61.7**	**1,596.4**	**38.3**	**4,171.1**

Source: Bureau of Economic Analysis (2012). NIPA Tables 3.2 and 3.3, last updated March 29, 2012. Note: Total government receipts exclude transfers received by state and local governments from the federal government. In 2011, these transfers totaled $492.5 billion in grants-in-aid and $71.4 billion in investment grants.

Table 5.2. U.S. Government Receipts (federal, state, and local), 2011

In addition to the above sources of revenue, it is possible for the federal government to finance expenditures by printing money. To be sure, the U.S. Congress or the administration does not have the authority to print money. Only the Fed, which is technically an independent entity, can increase the money supply.

This can happen in two ways.

First, the Fed can print new currency to put into circulation (although actual printing takes place at the U.S. Bureau of Engraving and Printing, which is part of the Department of the Treasury).

Second, and more common, is an "open market operation." To raise the money supply, the Fed buys back Treasury bonds from private banks and pays them by raising their reserve balances at the Fed, which the banks can then use to lend to other banks and businesses. This increase in the money supply typically leads to inflation if the growth rate of the money supply exceeds the growth rate of the economy—too much money chasing too few goods!

In the United States, this is an important difference between state governments and the federal government, which we define here to include the Fed. Since the Fed can "monetize the debt" by turning Treasury bonds into money, thereby creating inflation, federal debt carries an additional risk. This is the risk of inflation.

High inflation makes it more difficult for consumers and businesses to make sound economic decisions, as the signaling function of the price system fails. When the price of a good rises, it becomes difficult to understand whether it is because consumers are demanding more of it or because all prices are rising with inflation. As a result, more workers and capital may go into the production of the good inefficiently. High inflation also comes with variable inflation, and this causes credit markets to disappear, making it impossible for businesses to fund their operations and for consumers to purchase durables.

Since inflation is a general rise in prices of goods and services, when inflation is high, consumers' income usually falls behind, and consumers are unable to buy as many goods as they could under low inflation. With inflation, money loses its purchasing power.

Historically, some governments have simply printed money to cope with severe economic troubles and engineered spectacular inflations. Examples include Germany and Hungary after both World Wars, Argentina and Brazil in the 1980s, and Zimbabwe in 2008. These economies experienced hyperinflation (with monthly inflation rates above 50%) and suffered devastating effects on the consumers who saw the purchasing power of their income and savings decline precipitously. Facing immense uncertainty about inflation and interest rates, businesses stopped hiring and making investments. These massive inflations resulted from huge budget deficits that could not be eliminated in time. Indeed, the biggest factor in establishing price stability in these economies was reforming the fiscal side first, with reductions in government spending and increases in the tax base.

In less turbulent times, inflation, as well as inflation expectations, leads to lower investment, misallocation of resources, and redistribution of wealth from savers to borrowers.

Economists have long understood the importance of an independent Fed, free of political pressure from the fiscal authorities. It is this independence that has allowed central banks around the world to succeed in keeping inflation low and stable over the past three decades.

However, the Fed has responded to the recent recession and financial crisis with a massive asset purchase (Treasury bonds and toxic assets like mortgage-backed securities, credit debt swaps, and agency debt) and increased the reserve balances of major financial institutions at the Fed to record levels. This has created fears of inflation.

Many analysts believe that the Fed will be able to act in time to shrink its balance sheet and not allow for high inflation in the U.S. Nevertheless, it is hard to deny the attractiveness of the inflation option, because it mitigates the real debt obligations of the federal government. In fact, Reinhart and Rogoff (2010) report that debt-to-GDP levels over 90% are linked to significantly higher inflation rates than what we have historically experienced in the United States.

While inflation in the U.S. is currently low, some of the regional Fed presidents warn that utmost care must be given to keeping the inflation rate at its target of 2%.

Returning now to the differences between state and federal governments: Unlike the federal government, almost all states have some form of balanced budget amendment in their constitutions. This requirement usually refers to operating budgets, while state capital expenditures (for highways, buildings, land, etc.) are largely financed by debt. Issuance of debt at the state level requires approval of the legislature or the voters. In addition, an important difference between state governments and the federal government lies in the inability of state governments to influence the money supply.

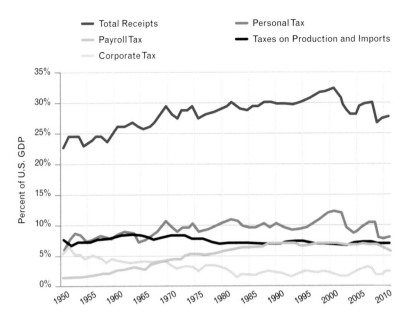

Source: Bureau of Economic Analysis (2012). NIPA Table 3.1, last revised March 29, 2012.

Figure 5.1. Components of U.S. Government Receipts as a Percentage of GDP, 1950–2011

TRENDS IN U.S. GOVERNMENT RECEIPTS

The most important historical trend in government tax revenue is the growth of payroll taxes, which more than tripled from 1950 to 2010. With projected aging of the population and increases in Social Security outlays and public health expenditures, payroll taxes will increase even more.

Let's take a look at the historical trends in the major categories of government receipts as a percentage of U.S. GDP since 1950. According to *Figure 5.1*, there is an upward trend in the ratio of total receipts to GDP between 1950 and 2000, which is largely driven by the increase in payroll taxes and, to a lesser extent, personal income taxes. However, since 2000, the trend in government receipts has reversed, mainly due to lower revenue collected from personal taxes. Total receipts of the government were 23% of GDP in 1950, peaked at 32% in 2000, and declined to 27% in 2011. The largest category of government receipts is the revenue collected from personal income taxes, which were 6.4% of GDP in 1950, peaked at 12.4% in 2000, and declined to 9.3% by 2011.

The category of tax receipts that displays the most significant increase over time is payroll taxes. These are the revenues obtained under the category of "contributions for government social insurance." Revenues from this source support expenditures on programs such as Social Security, Medicare, unemployment insurance, and disability insurance. Payroll taxes increased from 1.9% of GDP in 1950 to 7.2% of GDP by 1992, where they remained until 1995. Since 1995, payroll taxes and taxes on production and imports have remained fairly constant, each at about 7% of GDP.

Revenues from corporate income taxes exhibit a downward trend, falling from 6.1% in 1950 to 1.9% by 1982. Since the early 1980s, corporate income taxes have ranged between 2% and 3% of GDP, but dipped below 2% in the 2001 and 2008 recessions.

The trend in tax receipts can be seen more clearly in *Figure 5.2*, where we isolate the total government tax-revenue-to-GDP ratio over time. Total tax revenue in *Figure 5.2* is the sum of personal taxes, taxes on production and imports, corporate taxes, and contributions for government social insurance (i.e., payroll taxes) shown in *Figure 5.2*, plus taxes from the rest of the world.

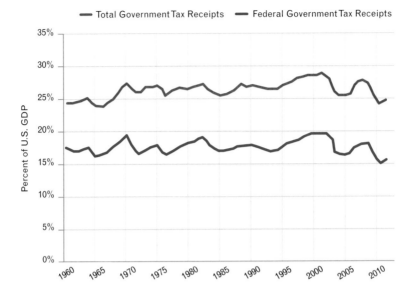

Source: Bureau of Economic Analysis (2011). NIPA Tables 3.1 and 3.2, last revised July 29, 2011.

Figure 5.2. U.S. Total Government Tax Receipts as a
Percentage of GDP, 1950–2010

Total tax collection increased from a level of about 24% in the 1960s to about 29% of GDP in 1999 and 2000. With the George W. Bush tax cuts, we see a reduction in the 2000s, which brought this ratio down to about 25% in 2003. Tax receipts increased again as the economy grew between 2003 and 2007, but declined in 2008 and 2009, primarily due to the Great Recession.

Looking at the ratio of federal tax receipts to GDP alone, we see a similar pattern. *Figure 5.2* depicts the ratio of federal tax receipts to GDP between 1960 and 2010. This ratio fluctuated around 18% until 1992, rose substantially under the Clinton administration to just over 20% in 2000, and declined to its historical levels during the George W. Bush administration. Receipts remained below historical levels, at 15% and 16% of GDP, in 2010 and 2011, respectively.

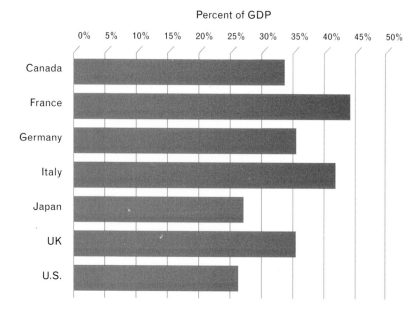

Percent of GDP

Source: OECD.StatExtracts (2011c). Revenue Statistics–Comparable Tables, data extracted on April 6, 2011.

Figure 5.3. Tax Revenues as a Percentage of GDP by Country,
2000–2009 average

LEARNING FROM OTHER COUNTRIES

Governments in rich European countries tax their citizens at a much higher level than the U.S. does. *Figure 5.3* shows average tax revenues between 2000 and 2009 as a percentage of GDP in Canada, France, Germany, Italy, the United Kingdom, Japan, and the United States.[24] (Japan, incidentally, has a ratio very similar to that of the United States, owing to the fairly low levels of personal income taxation in Japan.)

---

24 Data for 2009 were not available for Japan.

There is a huge difference in taxation levels across European countries and the United States. According to OECD data, the average tax burden in the United States over the past decade is just under 27%, whereas the averages in France and Italy are over 40%.

Put differently, for every euro of national income generated in these European countries, 40% goes to the government and the rest to private consumption and investment. Regardless of the quantity and quality of services provided by the public sector, the fraction of resources that European governments extract from their economies is very large.

However, it should be noted that these wealthy nations (like France and Germany) provide considerably more government services per capita than the U.S. does. Or put another way, the U.S. provides "less" government yet has a more indebted government than many European countries. The Europeans have higher taxes, and overall, they also squeeze out much more from those taxes.

KEY TAKE-AWAYS

Given the excess of total spending over total receipts, the U.S. government has had persistent budget deficits, adding to the existing stock of debt, which stood at 68% in 2011.

Total expenditures of the U.S. government were 38% and 37.3% of GDP in 2010 and 2011, well above their historical average of 33% between 1980 and 2007. With tax revenues at historical lows, this situation has created very large budget deficits.

The two largest spending items in the U.S. total government budget are social transfer payments (Social Security, Medicare, etc.) and government consumption (national security and education). These two components totaled 33% of GDP in 2010. Historically, consumption expenditures averaged 16% of GDP but rose to 17% in 2010 and

2011 due to increased national security spending.

Transfer payments were about 5% of GDP in the 1950s and 1960s, but have increased steadily over the past 50 years and reached 12.6% of GDP by 2007 and 15.7% by 2011. The driving force behind this growth was the increased coverage of Social Security programs and the establishment of Medicare and Medicaid programs by the Social Security Act of 1965. As the U.S. population is projected to age and live longer, larger proportions of the population (baby boomers) will become net recipients of transfer payments; consequently, transfer payments are expected to grow prodigiously larger.

While total expenditures were 37.3% of GDP in 2011, total receipts were 27.6% of GDP, which is lower than the average 30% historically observed between 1980 and 2007. The main sources of such tax receipts are taxes on personal income and contributions for social insurance (payroll taxes). The latter category displays the most significant increase over time, growing from 1.9% of GDP in 1950 to hovering around 7% since the late 1980s. Revenues from this source support expenditures on programs such as Social Security, Medicare, unemployment insurance, and disability insurance.

The projected growth in transfer payments (due to aging, increased coverage, and increasing relative prices) clearly suggests that the current fiscal situation is not sustainable. According to some projections by the CBO, the U.S. debt will exceed 100% of GDP by 2021.[25]

If the U.S. cannot quickly and drastically reduce our ballooning transfer payments and government purchases (while simultaneously increasing our tax revenues), we can expect budget deficits and debt so large that the economy will shrink (by up to 6%) by 2025.

---

25 CBO (2011a).

CHAPTER 6

GOVERNMENT'S IMPACT ON THE ECONOMY

When a household wants to reduce its debt, it needs to spend less or earn more. Higher household income is a good thing; it allows debt reduction and possibly higher consumption spending.

A debt-ridden government is similar to a household with debt. To reduce its debt, the government needs to spend less or raise its income.

However, the similarity ends there. When the government raises its income, it must take money away from households. This cannot be a good thing.

How do individuals respond when they face higher taxes? How does the economy react to higher taxes?

Here, we provide economic evidence (and intuition) on this issue.

We also explore whether popular concerns about high debt levels, which often result from increased "deficit financing" (when government bond issues are used to finance expenditures) during times of recession or war, are justified.

Deficit financing provides the government with increased flexibility and is often preferable to an increase in current taxes. However, there is some evidence that, above a certain threshold, high debt levels (relative to GDP) slow economic growth and can stoke inflation. A related concept is whether a similar threshold exists for the size of government spending relative to GDP.

We first consider the impact of taxes on labor and capital inputs. Then we examine some of the advantages and disadvantages of increased deficit financing, and explore what level of debt-to-GDP ratio may be acceptable.

TAXES

When the government raises taxes or borrows and creates the expectation of future tax increases, the behavior of individuals and businesses changes, affecting GDP.

It is easy to imagine that economic activity will be curtailed when individuals and businesses face higher tax rates. If, for example, the government takes 90% of every additional dollar that I earn, I will not have much of an incentive to work longer hours or try to do any additional work. It is, however, more difficult to quantify the exact reaction of all the individuals in an economy as tax rates are increased to 30% or 50%. The same principles apply, and economic activity will be curtailed, but by how much? The exact amount is very important, since it determines the size of the pie, the U.S. GDP!

In general, economics literature finds that current taxes are important because of their effects on the economic behavior of individuals and businesses.

First, changes in current taxes directly affect employment and saving. Higher private saving raises the supply of loanable funds and the amount of capital in the economy. Since labor and capital are two of the most important determinants of national income, changes in these factors result in changes in GDP. Thus, taxes indirectly affect GDP and economic growth through their impact on labor supply and capital investment.

Second, these changes in behavior have consequences for the total amount of tax revenues that are collected, because tax revenues are a function of not only tax rates but also the tax base. The tax base consists of taxpayers' wages, taxpayers' consumption, and businesses' profits. Thus, the tax base depends on the behavior of taxpayers. Consequently, to generate reasonable estimates for tax revenues, one must take into account how taxpayers will respond to changes in tax rates. Will higher income or payroll or sales tax rates affect individuals' incentives to work or purchase goods and services? Will employers respond to higher payroll taxes by hiring fewer people? Will higher taxes on capital gains result in lower investment?

The term "taxes" is a general one. The reality is that the impact of taxes on the economy depends on the type of tax and the government programs that the collected tax revenues fund.

Changes in tax rates create inefficiencies—also referred to as "distortions"—that must be taken into account. Businesses and individuals need to know what taxes will be today and in the future to plan their hiring and spending decisions. Tax distortions arise when tax rates are increased, because this leads businesses and individuals to make choices that are different (and worse) from those they would prefer to make.[26]

In addition, expectations about future taxes distort the economic behavior of individuals and firms. Given the distortions created by taxes, it is well known that the most efficient way for governments to collect revenues is through one-time, lump-sum taxation. However, because such taxes are often neither available nor politically desirable, governments use a combination of capital, labor, and consumption (i.e., sales) taxes to collect revenues. In the sections that follow, we summarize some of the current research that examines the effect of labor and capital taxes, in particular, on labor supply and capital accumulation.

TAXATION AND LABOR

The majority of U.S. government revenues are obtained from taxes on labor.

In 2010, 30% of government revenues was generated through personal income taxes and 24.9% was generated through payroll taxes. Hence, 54.9% of government revenues was obtained through taxing labor income.

The proportion of total tax revenue raised by these two taxes has increased significantly over the past few decades. For example, between 1950 and 2010, these two taxes rose from 37% of government revenues to 55% of government revenues, and this trend is expected to continue in the future.

What are the effects of increases in personal and payroll taxes on the behavior of labor markets?

Theoretically, a change in personal income or payroll (Social Security) taxes affects an individual's after-tax wage rate, which generates two opposing effects, namely, an "income effect" that provides workers with an incentive to work more and a "substitution" effect that provides workers with an incentive to work less.

If the after-tax wage rate declines, individuals who now have less income will reduce their consumption of goods and services, as well as leisure activities, and increase the number of hours they work in an effort to make up for their reduced after-tax income. This is the "income effect" of taxes.

But simultaneously, a decline in the after-tax wage rate reduces the reward from working, which discourages work effort.[27, 28] So a drop in after-tax wage rates provides individuals with an incentive to reduce the number of hours they work in the legal labor market sector and spend more time instead on untaxed activities—leisure, home production,[29] and other nonmarket (noncash) activities. This is the "substitution effect."

---

26 Taxes will cause businesses and individuals to roll back their plans to hire, invest, work, and consume.

27 In this discussion, the opportunity cost of leisure is the amount of after-tax wages forgone when one chooses to work less or not at all. If the income tax rate increases, the after-tax wage rate, and thus the opportunity cost of leisure, decreases.

28 Since payroll taxes are essentially flat up to a certain income level and zero afterward, distortions they create are smaller than those created by personal income taxes, which are progressive (i.e., the individual pays a larger fraction of each dollar of income as his or her earnings increases).

29 Home production refers to activities, such as child rearing or cooking, that are done at home without receiving an explicit payment.

If the substitution effect is stronger than the income effect, then individuals may choose to work less if taxes increase. This would reduce the overall supply of labor in the economy, which would have negative consequences for GDP and economic growth. Evidence from European countries suggests that higher taxes could indeed have such a "disincentive effect" on labor behavior. For example, Nobel laureate Edward C. Prescott found that higher tax rates in certain European countries relative to the United States accounted for the lower number of hours worked in these countries relative to the U.S.[30]

However, the disincentive effect of higher taxes on work effort also depends on how the government chooses to spend its tax revenues. Studies suggest that even though they face similar high tax rates, workers in Scandinavian countries work more hours than those in the rest of Europe. Despite high tax rates, the disincentive effect of taxes on labor supply is muted in countries where the government spends its income tax revenues on benefit programs tied to labor market participation.

Research in this area tries to quantify the effect of taxes on individuals' incentives to work. One facet of this research attempts to quantify the responsiveness of labor supply to changes in after-tax wage rates, a measure known as "labor supply elasticity."

A clear understanding of this issue is very important. If tax rates are raised in the near future to reduce our national debt, how much will this increase reduce incentives to work and create jobs?

THE EFFECT OF LABOR TAXES ON LABOR SUPPLY

Can differences in labor income tax rates between European countries and the United States explain why individuals in Europe work fewer hours than American workers?

Edward C. Prescott thinks so. In his 2004 article, Prescott argues that differences in total hours worked between the U.S. and some larger European countries in the 1970–1974 and 1993–1996 periods can be explained by the difference in their tax rates. We highlight some of the data used by Prescott in *Table 6.1*.

	HOURS PER WEEK PER PERSON		1993-1996	
	1970–1974	1993–1996	GDP per Hour (as % of U.S.)	GDP per Person (as % of U.S.)
Germany	24.6	19.3	99	74
France	24.4	17.5	110	74
Italy	19.2	16.5	90	57
Canada	22.2	22.9	89	79
UK	25.9	22.8	76	67
Japan	29.8	27.0	74	78
U.S.	23.5	25.9	100	100

Source: Prescott (2004).

Table 6.1. Hours Worked per Person, Productivity, and GDP per Person

30 Prescott (2004).

81

The second and third columns of *Table 6.1* contain information on the labor input, measured as hours worked per person, in the early 1970s versus the early 1990s. The third column presents average labor productivity, measured as GDP per hour, in these countries relative to GDP per hour in the United States, and the last column presents GDP per person in each country relative to GDP per person in the United States—both for the 1993–1996 period.

Several observations from *Table 6.1* are worth highlighting. First, Americans worked much more than Europeans in the 1993–1996 period. These data indicate that Americans worked 34% more than Germans, 48% more than the French, 57% more than Italians, and 13% more than Canadians and the British.

Second, this was not always the case. In fact, in the early 1970s, Americans worked fewer hours than Germans, the French, the British, and the Japanese. Hours per week were 24.4 in France, 24.6 in Germany, and 23.5 in the United States. This observation makes invoking cultural differences to explain the differences in hours worked in the 1990s unconvincing. This dramatic change in European and American work hours provides a possibility for examining the importance of labor market institutions while abstracting from cultural differences.

The fourth column in *Table 6.1* presents data on GDP per person in each country relative to the United States in the early 1990s. According to these data, GDP per capita in Germany and France was 74% of U.S. GDP in the early 1990s. Canada and Japan were at almost 80% of U.S. levels, and Italy was at about 60%.

What is the reason for the significant differences in levels of per capita GDP (which is a proxy for living standards) attained across these countries in the early 1990s? Does the answer lie in differences in productivity across countries? For example,

82

are workers in the United States more productive, do they produce more per hour worked, than workers in Germany?

Column 4 displays data on average labor productivity in this period measured as output per hour worked. Except for Japan and the United Kingdom, labor productivity across these countries is more similar to that of the United States than their levels of output per person. In other words, differences in GDP per person do not seem to stem from differences in average labor productivity (GDP per hour). Given that output per person in these countries (excluding Japan and the UK) does not differ markedly from output per person in the United States, any differences in per capita output must stem from differences in hours worked. But what explains the dramatic differences in hours worked across these countries, as well as within these countries over these two time periods?

Prescott (2004) concludes that differences in tax policies across these countries are capable of explaining the observed differences in hours worked. *Figure 6.1* illustrates the negative relationship between effective marginal tax rates and productivity over these two periods, 1970–1974 and 1993–1996.[31] As shown in *Figure 6.1*, in the early 1970s, when tax rates were relatively similar between the United States and European countries, their hours worked were also similar. By the 1990s, tax rates in Europe had increased. According to the calculations in Prescott (2004), marginal tax rates on income from labor in Germany, France, and Italy were about 60% in the early 1990s, as opposed to 40% for the United States. Such differences in taxes can account for the differences in hours worked when comparing the U.S., Germany, and France.

---

31 Prescott (2004) combines labor and consumption tax rates into a single tax rate, which he calls the "effective marginal tax rate on labor income."

Source: Prescott (2004).

Figure 6.1. Hours Worked vs. the Effective Tax Rate

A popular explanation for differences in hours worked across countries is cultural differences. While cultural differences may be important across countries, it is striking to show that differences in taxes can account for differences in hours worked relatively easily. In terms of welfare, which measures the total utility or well-being of the individuals in an economy, these results are very significant. According to these estimates, if France were to reduce its taxes on labor income to the U.S. level, the welfare (utility) of French workers would increase by 19%.[32]

A critical assumption underlying Prescott's work is that all tax receipts are distributed lump-sum back to households, based on the idea that public goods are good substitutes for private consumption (e.g., public schools and hospitals are good substitutes for private schools and hospitals).

84

This assumption is important for generating a large response of labor supply to tax changes, as it practically eliminates the income effect of taxes, which causes individuals to work more.

Others have criticized this approach. For example, Ljungqvist and Sargent (2006) argue that differences in policies such as social security, unemployment insurance, and disability are more important in explaining differences in hours worked across countries than differences in tax policies.

The study by Prescott (2004) sparked a substantial amount of research into the differences in labor behavior across countries. Subsequent work by Rogerson (2006) and Ohanian, Raffo, and Rogerson (2008) examined a sample of 21 OECD countries between 1956 and 2003 and between 1956 and 2004, respectively, and reinforced Prescott's findings. Ohanian, Raffo, and Rogerson show that there was a significant decrease in the average hours of work in this group of countries between 1956 and 2004. Their findings indicate that differences in tax rates are able to account for this decline, as well as most of the variation in hours worked across these countries.

In general, countries where marginal tax rates increased experienced a decrease in hours worked over time, which led to lower levels of GDP per capita.[33]

---

32 Welfare is measured by lifetime consumption equivalents, which is the current value of an increase in lifetime consumption for a 22-year-old.

33 Using data for 19 countries, Davis and Henrekson (2005) show that higher tax rates on labor income and consumption expenditures lead to not only less work time in the market sector but also more work time in the household sector and a bigger underground economy, as the theory would suggest. In particular, countries with relatively high tax rates experience a disproportionately lower employment in those market activities that have good nonmarket substitutes.

There are, however, some notable exceptions. Hours worked in Scandinavian countries (Denmark, Finland, Norway, and Sweden) remained high despite the presence of high tax rates. In particular, hours of work relative to the United States were about 82% in Scandinavian countries and 68% in Continental Europe (Belgium, France, Germany, and Italy) in 2003. Hours worked in both of these groups of countries, however, were 10% higher than in the United States in 1959.

In other words, Scandinavian countries experienced a much smaller decline in hours worked between 1959 and 2003 than countries in Continental Europe. Yet during the same time period, tax rates increased by more in Scandinavian countries than in Continental Europe.

Some economists argue that the way governments spend their revenues collected from labor taxes has important effects on the labor supply response.[34] Rogerson (2007) finds that if tax revenues are used to fund programs that depend on individuals working, such as subsidized care for children or the elderly or payments for child care that are conditional on being gainfully employed, then the disincentive effects of taxes on labor behavior are muted. This positive linkage between working and eligibility for benefits funded by tax revenues may explain why hours worked in Scandinavian countries are high relative to those in Continental Europe, despite their similarly higher tax rates.

Scandinavian governments spend much more money on family care than Continental European ones. Government spending on these services is about 8% of total spending for Scandinavian countries, compared with about 2% in Continental Europe.[35]

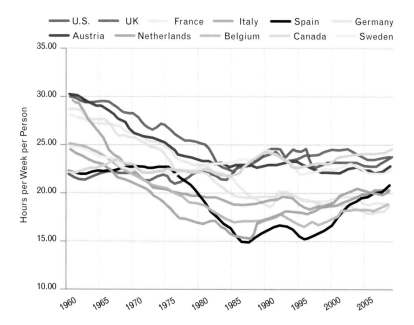

Source: OECD.StatExtracts (2011b).

Figure 6.2. Average Hours Worked per Week, 1960–2006

Notice that government transfers that depend on individuals' not working also exist, such as unemployment insurance or social security. Increases in such programs have negative effects on hours worked.

In *Figure 6.2*, we provide data on average hours worked per week for Austria, Belgium, Canada, France, Germany, Italy, the Netherlands, Spain, Sweden, the United Kingdom, and the

34 Rogerson (2007) points out that this observation does not weaken the validity of the strong relationship between taxes and hours worked discussed.

35 Ragan (2005).

United States between 1960 and 2006.[36] This is a much smaller sample than used in some of the studies summarized so far but will help illustrate a number of the points made in these studies.

Striking differences between hours worked in the United States and in this sample of countries are quite apparent.

First, all countries, except for the United States and Canada, experienced significant declines in average hours worked over this time period.

Second, in 1960, average hours worked in most countries were higher than in the United States. In fact, average hours worked remained higher in Austria, France, Germany, and the United Kingdom until the 1980s. As mentioned earlier, this observation suggests that relying on cultural differences to explain differences in hours worked may not be very fruitful.

EFFECTIVE LABOR INCOME TAX RATES AND LABOR SUPPLY

The United States government is running high budget deficits, raising the already-high debt-to-GDP ratio, and creating expectations of higher future tax rates. In addition to labor income taxes, some politicians are also talking about value added or consumption taxes.

We must examine how American companies and workers will react to the prospect of higher taxes in the future.

In this section, we study the impact of effective tax rates (defined as a combination of personal tax rates, payroll tax rates, and property and sales tax rates) on economic activity.

Many factors may be responsible for the observations made about hours worked in *Figure 6.3*. But how about the role of changes in taxes? Can we glean any relationship between taxes and hours worked examining the cross-country evidence?

Examining the cross-country experience may help understand how the U.S. workers and firms may behave if they are faced with higher taxes.

Figure 6.3 displays the average effective tax rates used in many of the studies summarized so far (for the same set of countries in *Figure 6.2*). *Figure 6.3* illustrates that there are significant differences in tax rates across countries.

In 1960, the effective tax rate ranged from a low of about 17% in Austria to a high of 38% in France. In fact, Austria is the only country that had a lower average effective tax rate than the United States until the mid-1980s. In addition, most countries in this sample experienced a dramatic increase in the average effective tax rate over this time period. By 2006, the effective tax rate was 26% in Austria and above 50% in Belgium, France, Germany, Italy, the Netherlands, and Sweden. It is these dramatic differences in tax rates across countries that motivated researchers to explore the role of taxes in accounting for differences in labor supply behavior.

---

36 Average hours worked per week is constructed as total hours of work divided by the product of the size of the population ages 15–64 and 52 weeks. Total hours of work are constructed as the product of civilian employment and annual hours of work per person in employment. Data for civilian employment and population ages 15–64 are obtained from the OECD.StatExtracts (2011b). The series for annual hours worked per person in employment comes from the Groningen Growth and Development Centre.

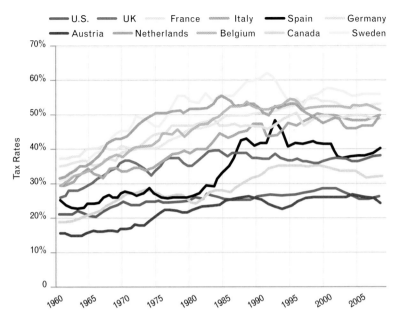

Source: McDaniel (2011).

Figure 6.3. Average Effective Tax Rates

While we recognize that simple correlations between two variables are often not very instructive, it is interesting to explore the relationship between the changes in taxes and the changes in the average number of hours worked depicted in *Figures 6.1* and *6.2*.

Table 6.2 shows that hours worked decreased as the effective tax rate increased. It presents data for 1960 and 2000, as well as the changes in the effective tax rate and the percentage change in hours worked that took place between these two years by country. Notice that the United States and Canada are the only countries in this sample that experienced an increase in average hours worked per week: 12% and 10%, respectively. All other countries experienced significant declines in average hours worked. The simple correlation between the changes in tax rates and the percentage change in hours worked is -0.23, providing empirical evidence of a negative relationship between the two. In short, *Table 6.2* indicates that even if tax rates rise, government revenues may not, because labor supply (or the tax base) may simultaneously shrink.

	Effective Tax Rate			Hours Worked per Week per Person		
	1960	2000	% Change	1960	2000	% Change
Austria	0.17	0.27	63.36	29.93	22.54	-24.69
Belgium	0.31	0.53	73.50	24.99	18.08	-27.65
Canada	0.20	0.36	79.31	21.75	23.95	10.13
France	0.38	0.54	42.79	28.02	19.48	-30.48
Germany	0.36	0.51	39.24	28.75	18.52	-35.59
Italy	0.31	0.51	64.93	29.99	19.26	-35.76
Netherlands	0.32	0.50	54.65	24.39	20.08	-17.66
Spain	0.26	0.39	48.84	22.10	18.64	-15.65
Sweden	0.32	0.58	82.93	24.75	23.02	-6.99
UK	0.27	0.39	42.73	29.98	23.21	-22.58
U.S.	0.22	0.29	34.17	21.84	24.50	12.21

Source: McDaniel (2011).

Table 6.2. Changes in Hours Worked and Effective Tax Rates

Most of the papers we examined have focused on the role of taxes in explaining the cross-country differences in hours worked. While this one factor alone is remarkably important in accounting for differences across countries in hours worked, other factors also deserve mention.

First, note that average hours worked in the United States and Canada increased despite small increases in the effective average tax rates during this period. Prescott (2004) argues that most of the increase in average hours worked between the early 1970s

91

and 1990s in the United States was due to the increased hours of work by married women.

Factors that led to a reallocation of time from the home sector into the market sector are also very important, especially in understanding the labor supply behavior of women. For example, changes in marginal tax rates that apply to married couples may be important in explaining such changes.

Second, the United States experienced rapid technological change in the 1990s, which may have contributed to the increase in hours worked despite some increases in taxes.

Third, there are significant differences across countries in other labor market regulations that are important to consider when examining hours worked.

Fourth, studies find that not only the level of taxes but also the type of programs that are supported by government revenues influences the incentives for work. If tax revenues are spent on programs that are tied to labor market participation of individuals, the disincentive effect of taxes is muted.

Nevertheless, this body of research suggests that there are significant negative consequences of higher tax rates on hours worked. Therefore, any fiscal policy action that leads to an increase in government spending that in turn leads to an increase in taxes needs to consider this consequence.

THE ELASTICITY OF LABOR SUPPLY

A critical parameter in evaluating the effect of changes in tax rates on hours worked is "labor supply elasticity," which measures the responsiveness of hours worked to changes in the after-tax wage rate. For instance, if a 10% decrease in the after-tax wage rate resulted in a 1% decline in hours worked, the labor supply elasticity would be small (0.1). In such a case, the disincentive effect of taxes on labor supply would be small—i.e., despite higher taxes, the tax base would be unlikely to shrink significantly. Several government reports (including the projections by the CBO that will be discussed) rely on very small labor supply elasticity estimates in making predictions about the likely effects of taxes. For example, a Congressional Research Service report by Hungeford (2010) relies on elasticity estimates "close to zero."

However, estimates of labor supply elasticity depend critically on how they are derived. Estimates based on individuals' responses (using household or payroll data) typically range between 0.1 and 0.5, (i.e., a 10% decrease in the after-tax wage rate is estimated to decrease hours worked by between 1% and 5%). But these estimates, which are generally based on responses by prime-age males, may not be representative of the economy as a whole. According to Rogerson and Wallenius (2009), labor supply elasticity for the economy as a whole is much higher, in the 2.3-3.0 range.[37]

Therefore, the government's budget outlook depends critically on different assumptions about labor supply elasticity.

---

37 Rogerson and Wallenius (2009) employ a life-cycle labor supply model and show that changes in the size of tax and transfer policies imply changes in terms of employment to population ratios (extensive margin) and hours of work per person in employment (intensive margin).

TAXATION AND CAPITAL ACCUMULATION

Taxes on income from capital take many forms—including those levied on interest, dividends, and capital gains received by individuals, as well as on business profits. Capital income tax systems tend to be highly complex, since some types of capital income are harder to tax than others.

Capital income taxation distorts individual savings decisions. For example, if the tax rate on interest income increases, this will discourage private saving. If savings decline, then total loanable funds in an economy will be lower, resulting in higher interest rates. Since higher interest rates mean a higher cost of capital for businesses, their investment in capital goods will decline.

Less investment means slower capital accumulation. This is harmful for future economic growth.

The problem is that all forms of taxation are distortionary. Therefore, a basic problem of public finance is how to use taxes to collect revenue in the least distortionary way.

Consider first the distortions caused by taxes that reduce the return to savers. This includes the corporate income tax and the taxes paid by individuals on dividends, interest, capital gains, and bequests.

Corporate profits are typically taxed twice, first at the corporate level and then again at the individual level, when after-tax corporate profits are distributed as taxable dividend income to shareholders. Thus, despite decreases in both the corporate tax rate and personal income tax rates since the mid-1980s, such double taxation still significantly reduces the after-tax return on the investment of an individual saver who invests his savings in publicly traded stocks. Because these after-tax returns are used to finance future consumption (say, during retirement), taxes on capital gains and dividends (taxes on capital income) are analogous to taxes on future consumption, according to Judd (1985) and Chamley (1986). These economists argue that the capital income tax rate should optimally be zero, because it creates disincentives to save.

For example, 1995 Nobel laureate Robert E. Lucas Jr. (1990) estimates that eliminating capital income taxation will increase the U.S. capital stock by 35%. Over a 10-year period, such an increase would more than double the annual growth rate of U.S. capital stock.

Harvard University economist Martin Feldstein (2006) helps explain this issue further through a simple example: Imagine an economy where the return to saving in the absence of taxation is 10%. Consider an individual who saves $100 at age 45 to spend it 30 years later, at age 75. With a 10% annual return, $100 will grow to $1,745 in 30 years ($100 x $[1 + 10\%]^{30}$). If, instead, there is a 50% tax on capital income, the same $100 will grow to only $432 ($100 x $[1 + (1 - 50\%) \times 10\%]^{30}$).

In short, these calculations highlight how policies that decrease the after-tax return to capital (such as high tax rates on capital income) will result in lower savings and investment, and therefore lower the capital stock.

Conversely, policies that increase the after-tax return to capital, such as low tax rates on capital income and investment tax credits, will result in higher savings and therefore a higher capital stock. This will spur economic growth.

DEFICITS AND FUTURE TAXES

Government deficits arise as a result of a shortfall between government expenditures and revenues. When government expenditures exceed government receipts, this shortfall must be financed by borrowing money through newly issued debt.

A household that spends more than it earns borrows from private banks. A government borrows from its citizens and from foreigners by issuing bonds that will have to be repaid with interest at some future date. For example, the U.S. government issues U.S. Treasury bonds. National debt therefore comprises these accumulated promises to pay, which extend into the future.

A key economic and practical question is the effect of deficits and debt on economic activity. Is it harmful to run deficits and accumulate high levels of debt?

In this section, we discuss some of the advantages and disadvantages of deficit financing. We also consider recent empirical evidence from advanced economies that finds a negative correlation between debt-to-GDP levels above 90% and GDP growth rates. For the U.S., debt levels over 90% of GDP are linked to significantly higher inflation rates. Deficit spending enables a government to finance short-run differences between its expenditures and its revenues.

As discussed earlier, changes in taxes create important distortions in an economy. Consequently, it is not desirable to push tax rates up and down over time. This creates considerable uncertainty about future tax liabilities and makes it very difficult for businesses and households to plan for future investment and consumption.

There are two key advantages in running budget deficits and accumulating debt.

First, deficits and debt act as automatic stabilizers, dampening fluctuations in GDP. During recessions, more people apply for unemployment insurance benefits, and as a result, transfer payments rise. At the same time, with reduced incomes, tax revenues fall. As a result of higher government spending and lower tax revenues, the budget deficit is larger than otherwise, and this has to be financed by new government debt.

If the government were unable or unwilling to allow the deficit to rise during a recession, then it would have to curtail unemployment insurance benefit payments that would otherwise provide temporary income relief for the jobless, or it would have to raise taxes that would hurt job creation and investment exactly when they are needed.

Therefore, deficits and debt act as buffers that help dampen business fluctuations.

Second, when a government incurs a very large, temporary, and unexpected expenditure, such as a big war, large budget deficits and debt can be useful. The United States financed huge war expenditures during World War II mostly by running large budget deficits and borrowing from the public. The federal budget deficit reached about 12% of GDP, and the debt held by the public exceeded 100% of GDP.

After the war, government expenditures were reduced, the transition from wartime economy to peacetime economy created an investment boom, GDP rose quickly, and deficits declined rapidly, together with the debt-to-GDP ratio.

Had the U.S. government relied exclusively on higher taxes to finance World War II, this would have discouraged investment activity and job creation during the war, as high tax rates would have created the wrong incentives for investment and job creation. Deficit financing served the United States well in this difficult time period.

Given these advantages, should we be concerned about the current level of the U.S. federal budget deficit and increasing levels of debt (particularly in such a low-interest-rate environment)? What are some of the impacts of deficits and debt on the economy?

There are four major disadvantages of relying on large deficits and high debt to finance current spending.

First, national debt creates a burden on future generations that must pay the principal and interest on debt. This can happen only with higher taxes in the future, and that's why it's called a burden on our children and grandchildren.

If our debt were domestically held, and if all this were passed on to future generations as bequests (passed on to our children and grandchildren), then large debt might not be that burdensome.

In June 2011, the total outstanding government debt in the U.S. was equal to $14.3676 trillion. Debt held by the public totaled $9.7469 trillion.[38]

A bit more than half (54%) of our publicly held debt is held by U.S. citizens.[39] As this debt is passed from generation to generation, the bonds will also be passed from parents to children to grandchildren. So while future generations may face higher taxes to pay for the principal and interest on government bonds, they will also be the recipients of these principal and interest payments.

But the portion of the debt held by foreigners (46%) will, in effect, be repaid by future generations without their receiving the benefits.

Major foreign holders of U.S. Treasury securities are summarized in *Table 6.3.*[40] Among the foreign countries, China is the largest holder of U.S. government debt (12%). Future taxes on U.S. citizens will have to be raised to pay for principal and interest payments, a substantial portion of which will be received by foreign nationals.

	U.S. Dollars (Millions)	As a % Total Public Debt
China, mainland	1,165.5	11.96
Japan	911.0	9.35
UK	349.5	3.59
Oil Exporters	229.6	2.36
Brazil	207.1	2.12
Taiwan	153.4	1.57
Caribbean banking centers	140.5	1.44
Hong Kong	118.4	1.21
Russia	109.8	1.13
Switzerland	108.2	1.11
Canada	84.4	0.87
Other	921.8	9.46
Total foreign holdings	4,499.2	46.16
Total debt held by the public	9,746.9	100.00

Source: U.S. Department of the Treasury (2011b).

Table 6.3. Major Foreign Holders of U.S. Treasury Securities, June 2011

38 Data from U.S. Department of the Treasury (2011a) and U.S. Department of the Treasury (2011b). Economists typically consider the debt held by the public as their focal point instead of the gross federal debt, which includes debt issued to various federal government agencies in addition to debt held by the public.

39 U.S. Department of the Treasury (2011b).

40 Data available from: www.treasury.gov/resource-center/data-chart-center/tic/Documents/mfh.txt.

THE FISCAL CLIFF

A second disadvantage of large budget deficits is their potential impact on interest rates and, ultimately, the capital stock.

Many economists argue that the large amount of borrowing that the government must initiate as a result of its budget deficit increases the demand for loanable funds, potentially resulting in higher interest rates. Higher interest rates in turn may "crowd out" (reduce) private investment and capital accumulation by increasing the cost of funds. With a higher cost of capital, business may find it too expensive to borrow from private banks and forgo its planned purchase or rental of office space, factories, equipment, and software. These private investment expenditures can be smaller than otherwise, leaving future generations with a smaller stock of private capital (buildings, factories, equipment, etc.).

Since this capital stock is an important determinant of GDP, the decline in investment and capital accumulation will result in lower GDP in the future, creating lower living standards for future generations.

However, a critical part of this argument is the assumed relationship between increases in government debt and its effect on interest rates and national savings. According to an alternative view, there would at best be a small impact on interest rates.[41]

In addition, when the government runs a budget deficit, the economy may be in a weak state and businesses may reduce their investment plans. This reduction in the demand for loanable funds reduces the interest rate and counteracts the effect described above.

At the end of the day, whether interest rates rise or fall with large budget deficits is an empirical matter. Evidence from the United States over time and from other advanced economies shows no clear connection between budget deficits and interest rates.

A third disadvantage of deficit financing is that it can create perverse incentives for the government. Since U.S. debt is denominated in U.S. dollars, an increase in inflation will reduce the real debt payments made by the government. This might create an incentive to engineer inflation in order to reduce the real obligations of the U.S. government. If the government were to give in to this temptation, however, the credibility of the government would erode and expectations of future inflation would reduce the global value of the U.S. dollar and make it very difficult for the U.S. government to find buyers for its bonds.

Lastly, large budget deficits and the resulting high debt-to-GDP ratios raise fiscal sustainability concerns. Will the U.S. government have sufficient revenue in the future to cover interest and principal payments on its debt? In other words, increased debt obligations raise concerns about the government's ability to make good on its commitments.

If holders of U.S. Treasury bonds, especially foreign holders such as China and Japan, were to lose faith in the credibility of the U.S. government's fiscal policy, they could start shifting their portfolios away from the U.S.-dollar-denominated bonds,

---

41 The view that budget deficits have no impact on interest rates and private investment expenditures is known as the "Ricardian equivalence," named after the 19-century British economist David Ricardo. According to this view, a decrease in current taxes has the same impact on the economy as an equal increase in the government deficit. The logic behind this view is as follows: Imagine a $100 reduction in taxes today. Suppose the consumer buys $100 worth of government bonds today. When the government has to raise taxes tomorrow to pay the principal and interest on the $100 bond, the consumer has just enough to pay these higher taxes. A reduction in tax revenues reduces government (public) savings, while the investment of the additional $100 increases private savings. Net national savings remain unchanged. If the Ricardian equivalence holds, then consumers internalize the government's budget constraint and thus, the timing of taxes does not affect the economy. If most of the debt is held domestically and individuals have a strong bequest motive, then the impact of deficits on interest rates or the current account (difference between exports and imports) may be small.

and we would then see a serious financial crisis and the collapse of the U.S. dollar. Do we want to take this chance?

Given high debt levels, people may expect increases in future taxes, which will affect the economic decisions of individuals and businesses.[42] Alternatively, as the ratio of debt to GDP rises, the likelihood of default on the debt increases. Such concerns regarding the creditworthiness of the U.S. government were seen in August 2011 when Standard & Poor's downgraded the U.S. government's credit rating (for the first time in the history of the ratings) from AAA to AA+.

In addition, increased demand by the government for loanable funds may lead lenders to demand higher interest rates, which in turn would result in a higher percentage of future tax revenues being diverted from other government programs to pay interest on the debt.

To better understand issues related to the sustainability of government debt over time, consider the ratio of government debt to GDP. It will remain constant over time provided government debt grows at the same rate as the economy (the annual percentage change in the amount of debt outstanding is the same as the annual percentage change in GDP). If the level of government debt grows faster than GDP, then this ratio increases. Conversely, if debt grows slower than GDP, this ratio decreases.

What level of debt-to-GDP ratio is acceptable to the public? What does economic theory say about the sustainability of debt?

Unfortunately, there is no simple economic model that we can use to make a strong case for a particular range of values for debt-to-GDP that would make it sustainable. We therefore refer to historical evidence.

Until the recession of 2007–2009, the largest debt levels after World War II were reached during 1993–1995, when publicly held debt was about 49% of GDP. In 2001, the debt-to-GDP ratio fell to 33% as deficits grew at a slower rate than GDP.

But with the onset of the deep recession that started at the end of 2007, coupled with increases in the deficit and the slowdown of the U.S. economy, debt-to-GDP levels rose dramatically. In 2011, the U.S. publicly held debt-to-GDP ratio was about 70%.

CBO projections for the next 75 years in the U.S. show a serious deterioration of the government deficit and the resulting debt levels. The publicly held debt-to-GDP ratio is expected to have risen to around 74% by 2012 and continue increasing thereafter. Two different projections by the CBO would result in debt-to-GDP ratios between 84% and 187% by 2035.

As we mentioned above, economic theory provides limited help in determining what levels of debt may be of concern for a particular economy. It may even be possible to argue that in an environment with low interest rates, as in the United States since 2010, one should not be too concerned about the level of debt. A 2010 global study by Reinhart and Rogoff finds that a debt-to-GDP ratio below 90% has little or no impact on economic growth. However, median growth rates are 1% lower than the lower debt groups for debt-to-GDP ratios over 90%.[43]

42 See Auerbach (2009) for a detailed discussion of these issues.

43 Reinhart and Rogoff (2010) examine the longer-term macroeconomic implications of public and external debt financing using data for 44 countries.

103

Even a 1-percentage-point higher GDP growth rate would deliver a 48% higher level of living standards over 40 years. This is a large improvement; any reduction in the long-run growth of GDP will harm our way of life permanently.

Table 6.4 displays data for 20 countries from Reinhart and Rogoff (2010), grouped into four categories of debt-to-GDP ratios: below 30%; 30–60%; 60–90%; and above 90%. According to these findings, the average growth rate in economies with high debt-to-GDP levels (above 90%) was 1.7%, compared with 3.7% for economies with low debt-to-GDP ratios (below 30%).

In addition, for the United States, Reinhart and Rogoff find that debt levels over 90% of GDP are linked to significantly higher inflation rates. Overall, they conclude that debt-to-GDP levels above 90% may pose serious risks to an economy.

Real GDP Growth as the Level of Government Debt Varies: Selected Advanced Economies, 1790-2009 (annual percent change)

Country	Period	Central (Federal) Government Debt/GDP			
		Below 30%	30% to 60%	60% to 90%	90% and Above
Australia	1902-2009	3.1	4.1	2.3	4.6
Austria	1880-2009	4.3	3.0	2.3	n.a.
Belgium	1835-2009	3.0	2.6	2.1	3.3
Canada	1925-2009	2.0	4.5	3.0	2.2
Denmark	1880-2009	3.1	1.7	2.4	n.a.
Finland	1913-2009	3.2	3.0	4.3	1.9
France	1880-2009	4.9	2.7	2.8	2.3
Germany	1880-2009	3.6	0.9	n.a.	n.a.
Greece	1884-2009	4.0	0.3	4.8	2.5
Ireland	1949-2009	4.4	4.5	4.0	2.4
Italy	1880-2009	5.4	4.9	1.9	0.7
Japan	1885-2009	4.9	3.7	3.9	0.7
Netherlands	1880-2009	4.0	2.8	2.4	2.0
New Zealand	1932-2009	2.5	2.9	3.9	3.6
Norway	1880-2009	2.9	4.4	n.a.	n.a.
Portugal	1851-2009	4.8	2.5	1.4	n.a
Spain	1850-2009	1.6	3.3	1.3	2.2
Sweden	1880-2009	2.9	2.9	2.7	n.a.
UK	1830-2009	2.5	2.2	2.1	1.8
U.S.	1790-2009	4.0	3.4	3.3	-1.8
Average		3.7	3.0	3.4	1.7
Median		3.9	3.1	2.8	1.9
Number of Observations	2,317	866	654	445	352

Source: Reinhart and Rogoff (2010).
Notes: An "n.a." denotes no observations were recorded for that particular debt range. There are missing observations, most notably during the World War I and II years; further details are provided in the data appendices to Reinhart and Rogoff (2009) and are available from the authors. Minimum and maximum values for each debt range are shown in bold.Sources used in Reinhart and Rogoff (2009) include, among many others: International Monetary Fund, World Economic Outlook, OECD, World Bank, Global Development Finance.

Table 6.4. GDP Growth Rate vs. Government Debt

THE SIZE OF THE GOVERNMENT

In discussing the impact of the size of the government (measured in terms of government spending) on economic growth, economists acknowledge two opposing factors.

First, increases in some government expenditures, such as infrastructure, are likely to enhance economic growth by increasing the productivity of labor and capital. But the increases in taxation that are needed to finance such expenditures have a dampening effect on economic growth, due to the disincentive effects on labor.

According to the Harvard University economist Robert Barro (1991), the relationship between economic growth and government expenditures seems to be "nonmonotonic," i.e., economic growth does not always increase as government spending increases. Rather, in the early stages of economic growth, increases in the size of the government are likely to increase economic growth. As the government of a poor nation builds roads and ports, businesses can organize the supply chain better. Workers, trucks, trains, and ships can carry merchandise between the point of production and the marketplace for sale.

However, after some threshold of government spending (relative to GDP) is crossed, continued increases in the size of government are likely to reduce economic growth. Empirically, the exact location of this threshold is difficult to establish and may differ by country. Therefore, the empirical evidence of the growth effects of public expenditure as a share of GDP is generally inconclusive.

However, there are some interesting studies worth mentioning. For example, Fölster and Henrekson (2001) examine a group of rich OECD countries and find a negative relationship between government expenditure and growth. This is consistent with the theory that we should expect to find a negative effect in countries where the size of the government sector exceeds a certain threshold relative to GDP. Fölster and Henrekson find that "an increase of the expenditure ratio by 10 percentage points is associated with a decrease in the growth rate on the order of 0.7–0.8 percentage points."

Giavazzai and Pagano (1990) examine the effects of contractionary fiscal policies that were pursued to reduce government spending in some European countries in the 1980s (in order to deal with the large public debt that had accumulated over the 1970s). Keynesian economics would suggest that a contractionary fiscal policy would lead to a decline in domestic demand and an increase in unemployment.

However, another line of thinking may be important. This line focuses on the role of expectations. A reduction in the size of the government allows individuals to expect a lower share of government in GDP and, thus, lower taxes in the future. Giavazzai and Pagano show that in Denmark and Ireland in the 1980s, the second effect dominated, and reductions in the size of the government had expansionary effects.

Pursuing a similar idea, Alesina, Ardagna, Perotti, and Schiantarelli (2002) examine the effects of fiscal policy on business investment, using data for 18 OECD countries during 1960 and 1996. They find that increases in public spending increase labor costs and decrease firm profits. Consequently, private investment declines. Their estimates suggest that an increase of 1 percentage point in the ratio of government spending to GDP leads to a decrease in investment (as a share of GDP) of 0.15 percentage points.

These findings lend support to the association of fiscal contractions with higher growth, even in the very short run.

107

CHAPTER 7

MAKING TOUGH CHOICES

If the 2012 political stalemate over fiscal reform continues, where is the U.S. economy headed?

The deficit-to-GDP and debt-to-GDP ratios experienced since 2007 reflect several events that have impacted the U.S. economy. So far, we have examined how current levels of government revenues and expenditures compare with historical levels, and shown that current revenues are relatively low and current expenditures are very high. These imbalances between government outlays and revenues have occurred mostly due to the financial crisis and the severe recession of 2007–2009.

During the recession, tax revenues declined sharply and the government enacted significant spending programs that increased outlays. While some of these spending programs may be temporary in nature, several categories in the government budget, such as Social Security and Medicare, are expected to increase in size in the future. As a result, the recent increases in the budget deficit and debt levels are not likely to be temporary.

Below, we discuss two scenarios for future U.S. federal government revenues, spending, deficits, and debt. These scenarios were prepared by the CBO, which is charged with supplying Congress with "objective, nonpartisan, and timely analyses" to aid economic and budgetary decision making.

To this end, the CBO examines the budget and the long-run economic outlook and provides a "baseline," against which Congress may measure the effects of proposed changes in spending and taxes on the economy.[44] In preparing the baseline, the CBO is required by law to assume that current spending and revenue laws will remain unchanged. Thus, the baseline is viewed as the CBO's best assessment of the economy's impact on revenue and spending given existing laws, assuming that there is no major reform of any kind. In its alternative projection, the CBO assumes a different path for tax rates into the future that results in tax revenues that are much more in line with historical data.

In the next section, we examine these scenarios closely and identify the assumptions that drive most of the differences in the projected outcomes. In addition, we provide an alternative scenario that incorporates more realistic assumptions about the responsiveness of labor to changes in marginal tax rates.

CBO PROJECTIONS

Our starting point is the end of 2011, when the U.S. federal government deficit reached an alarming $1.299 trillion. In 2011, GDP was $15.176 trillion, producing a deficit-to-GDP ratio of 8.6%. The federal debt held by the public reached $10.127 trillion, giving us a debt-to-GDP ratio of 66.7% for 2011. Both the deficit and debt are at levels not seen since World War II.

The CBO has prepared two projections for the U.S. economy that yield vastly different long-run outcomes.

One scenario projects that by 2035, the deficit will be 4% of GDP and the amount of federal debt held by the public will be about 84% of GDP.

The other scenario projects that the deficit will be 16% of GDP and debt 187% of GDP by 2035.

What assumptions drive these dramatic differences? Which is the more realistic outcome? To answer these questions, we examine in detail the projections of revenues and expenditures underlying each scenario, consider the strengths and weaknesses of each, and generate some alternative views (in which it can get even worse!).

The Extended-Baseline Scenario: The assumptions used in this scenario are the most favorable (or optimistic) for producing smaller deficits for the U.S. economy.

On the revenue side, the projections result in tax revenue collections moving up from 15% of GDP in 2010 to 21% in 2020 and 23% in 2035.

On the spending side, the CBO assumes primary spending (all spending except the interest payments on federal debt) to be about 23% of GDP in 2011 and then fall to 20% by 2020. With these assumptions, the projected deficit would equal about

44 CBO (2011b).

4% of GDP in 2035, and federal debt held by the public would be around 84% of GDP in 2035 (with the figures projected to rise in the years after 2035, due to higher interest payments).

Note that this more favorable scenario does not come close to including budget surpluses that are sufficiently large to bring the debt-to-GDP ratio back to its historical levels of about 40%.

The Alternative Fiscal Scenario: In this alternative projection, the CBO assumes a different path for tax rates into the future that results in tax revenues as a percentage of GDP to increase from 2010's 15% to around 18% in 2020 and 2035.

These assumed tax rates are much more in line with historical data. The assumptions that led to the revenue projections under this scenario included the extension of the 2001 and 2003 tax cuts and the extension of the provisions designed to limit the reach of the alternative minimum tax.

On the spending side, the CBO assumes that the annual appropriations would keep pace with the growth of GDP. For example, spending on major mandatory health programs and interest payments are assumed to be at levels experienced during much of the past decade (under the extended-baseline scenario, they were assumed to fall below their historical levels).

Under these assumptions, CBO concludes that in 2020, the budget deficit will be growing steadily and that debt held by the public will have reached almost 97% of GDP by 2020 and 187% of GDP by 2035.

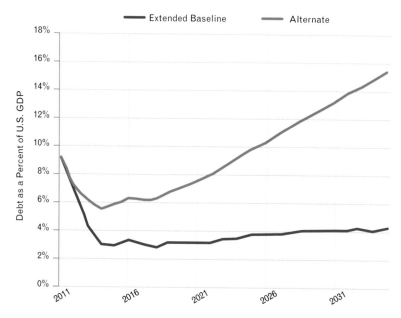

Source: Congressional Budget Office (2011c).

Figure 7.1. Deficit as a Percentage of GDP

Deficit projections for 2035 shown in *Figure 7.1* range from 4% of GDP under the extended-baseline scenario to 15% of GDP under the alternative fiscal scenario.

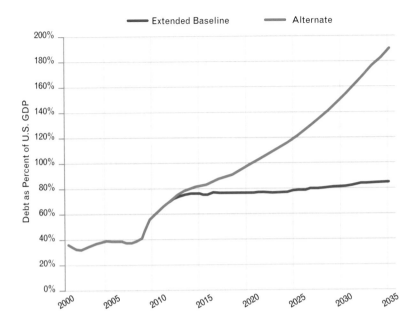

Source: Congressional Budget Office (2011c). Figure 1-2.

Figure 7.2. Debt as a Percentage of GDP

Debt projections displayed in *Figure 7.2* show the dramatic differences between the two scenarios up to 2035. Notice that the projected debt-to-GDP level of 80% under the baseline scenario is more than twice the historical levels. (The average debt-to-GDP ratio between 1960 and 2010 was 36.7%.)

As we will show, differences between the two scenarios are primarily driven by higher assumed tax rates under the extended-baseline scenario. However, even with the higher assumed tax rates and resulting tax revenues, the extended-baseline scenario projects continued deficits and relatively high debt levels, largely due to projected increases in health care expenditures.

UNDERLYING ASSUMPTIONS FOR
THE CBO PROJECTIONS

In this section, we examine more closely the assumptions and projections for expenditures and revenues underlying each of the CBO's two scenarios.

First, we consider CBO projections for the main components of federal government expenditures. Then we examine projected revenues. We show that differences between the two scenarios are primarily driven by higher projected tax rates and revenues under the extended-baseline scenario. Underlying their revenue projections is an assumption about the lack of distortions created by higher taxes. In other words, higher tax rates are assumed not to reduce labor supply or job creation at all.

Figure 7.3 presents projections for Social Security, health care (Medicare, Medicaid, the Children's Health Insurance Program, and exchange subsidies), and net interest expenditures as a percentage of GDP between 2011 and 2085 under the two CBO scenarios.

Expenditures on Social Security, shown in blue in *Figure 7.3*, are identical under the two scenarios and increase from 5% of GDP in 2011 to 6% in 2085. Health care expenditures rise much faster than Social Security expenditures, reaching 17% and 19% under these two scenarios by 2085.

However, the most striking difference comes from expenditures on net interest shown with the black and red lines in *Figure 7.3*.[45]

45 Net interest is interest payments less interest receipts.

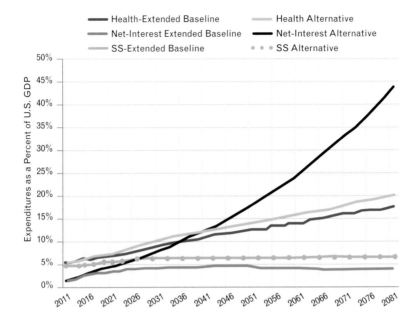

Source: Congressional Budget Office (2011c).

Figure 7.3. Expenditure Projections

Under the first scenario, net interest remains relatively flat, whereas under the second scenario, net interest spending rises significantly over time, surpassing all other expenditures by around 2040.

This increase is due to the higher rate of growth in debt held by the public under the second scenario. As the stock of debt accumulates, interest due on the outstanding debt increases to 43% of GDP by 2085 under the alternative fiscal scenario, compared with only 3.7% of GDP under the extended-baseline scenario.

Thus, the impact of continued accumulation of debt will be felt long into the future, in the form of higher interest payments, if the stock of debt is not reduced quickly.

If 43% of GDP is spent just on paying interest on the debt, the government will simply not have enough to spend on Social Security, health care, defense, education, and other essential categories.

The other major expenditure category is discretionary spending.[46]

CBO projections under both scenarios assume a decline in discretionary spending over time. In particular, noninterest discretionary spending as a percentage of GDP, which was 12.3% in 2011, is assumed to decline to 7.8% under the extended-baseline scenario and to 8.5% under the alternative fiscal scenario by 2035.[47]

Both of these levels are lower than the historical average of 8.7% between 1971 and 2010 and represent an optimistic view about the future of U.S. discretionary spending.[48]

It is also important to point out that CBO projections on spending are for the federal government only. However, state and local government consumption constitutes a large fraction of total government consumption in the U.S.

For example, in 2010, 58% of total government consumption spending was done by state and local governments. There are significant transfers from the federal government to the state

---

46 Discretionary programs are funded through the annual appropriation process. Major categories are expenditures on transportation, education, training, employment and social services, income security, health, veterans' benefits, and energy. Mandatory spending refers to government spending on programs that are required by law, such as Social Security, Medicare, Medicaid, and defense.

47 CBO (2011a).

48 CBO (2011a).

117

and local governments that enable these expenditures. CBO projections do not specifically deal with the difficulties that will be faced in reducing spending at the state and local levels.

Given that expenditures under the two scenarios are not drastically different (aside from net interest payments), why do net interest payments and the outstanding debt increase so much in the alternative fiscal scenario? Just what does the alternative fiscal scenario assume these borrowed funds are used to finance?

It assumes continued deficits due to revenues that fall short of expenditures, year after year. The main difference between the two scenarios lies in their projections for government revenues.

Figure 7.4 displays actual revenues between 1970 and 2010 and projected revenues through 2085 under the two scenarios, each as a percentage of GDP. Average revenues collected as a percentage of GDP between 1970 and 2010 were about 18%. However, according to the extended-baseline scenario, revenues as a percentage of GDP are projected to increase to 19.9% of GDP by 2014 and reach an unprecedented level of 30.6% of GDP by 2085.

The CBO assumes that these increases will be accomplished by increases in marginal tax rates on labor income, from 29% in 2010 to 35% in 2035.

However, such tax rate increases would likely have significant adverse consequences for the economy, stemming from the reaction of the labor supply.

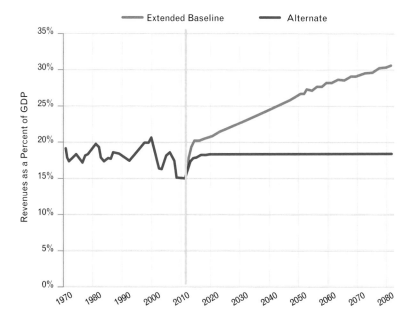

Source: Congressional Budget Office (2011c). Figure B-1.

Figure 7.4. Federal Government Revenues as a Percentage of GDP

Assumptions used for the extended-baseline scenario do not necessarily reflect the most likely outcomes for the U.S. economy. By comparison, tax revenue projections under the alternative fiscal scenario are more in line with historical levels. However, the alternative fiscal scenario results in continued budget deficits and extremely large debt-to-GDP ratios.

SHORTCOMINGS OF THE CBO PROJECTIONS

The CBO projections minimize the effect of changes in tax rates on labor supply, which is a significant shortcoming. The CBO projections assume that increases in marginal tax rates have a very small impact, if any, on people's incentives to work and businesses' incentives to create jobs. More specifically, in these projections, the average number of hours worked by

119

people in each demographic group remains unchanged, despite the fact that higher tax rates mean lower after-tax wages.

Thus, the CBO either assumes that the labor supply elasticity is close to zero or the CBO fails to consider the impact of taxes on labor supply behavior, which some studies, such as those reviewed in Chapter 2, suggest can be substantial.

Economists have extensively studied the extent to which labor supply responds to higher tax rates on income (i.e., the elasticity of labor supply).

Some studies find that increases in marginal tax rates lead to reductions (on a per capita basis) in hours worked and therefore GDP. And fewer hours worked and lower GDP mean a lower tax base, and hence lower tax revenues collected.

In fact, one study found that when higher tax rates affect work behavior negatively, the increase in total tax revenues is less than half as much as when increases in marginal tax rates elicit no behavioral response.[49]

It is therefore important to consider potential scenarios in which the labor supply does not remain constant in the face of such large changes in marginal tax rates. In fact, in the CBO's extended-baseline scenario, marginal tax rates on labor increase from about 25% in 2011 to 35% in 2035.[50] These are relatively large changes in marginal tax rates that would generate considerable reductions in labor supply and GDP, and also reduce tax revenues collected.

Thus, the extended-baseline scenario may overstate the tax revenue benefits of higher marginal tax rates, since no meaningful consideration is paid to how labor supply will respond. In the following section, we present several different scenarios for the

U.S. economy and examine the sensitivity of the CBO projections to certain assumptions, specifically concerning the impact of tax rates on labor supply and tax revenues.

ALTERNATIVE PROJECTIONS

Forecasting GDP is a challenging task, to say the least. But it is essential if we want to gauge the size of future deficits and debt, since both will be influenced by how the economy performs in the decades ahead.

One simple construct we can use is the Cobb-Douglas production function that was introduced in Chapter 3 (see pg. 135) as the basic building block of all economic models. It describes how GDP is produced as a combination of labor (total hours worked by all employees in the U.S.), capital (buildings, factories, offices, equipment, machines, computer software, etc.), and "total factor productivity" (TFP), which describes the collective influences of economic, social, and legal institutions on the economy.

---

49 Feldstein and Feenberg (1995) provide an interesting study of the effect of increases in marginal tax rates on tax revenues in the U.S. The authors examine the 1993 tax legislation that raised U.S. marginal tax rates from 31% to 36% on taxable incomes between $140,000 and $250,000 and to 39.6% on incomes above $250,000. Estimates of revenues that assume no labor response imply increased tax revenues of $19.3 billion. However, with the changes in behavior, they find that taxable income was lower than was the case under the no-response scenario and, although the total amount of taxes collected was higher because of higher tax rates, tax revenues increased only $8.8 billion. The increase in tax revenues was less than one-half of what it would have been with no behavioral response.

50 CBO (2011a).

	GNP	Total Hours	Capital Stock	TFP
1960-2010	3.13	1.47	2.96	1.05
1990-2010	2.54	0.72	2.54	1.09
1960-2007	3.31	1.72	3.06	1.04
1990-2007	2.95	1.28	2.74	1.06

Source: Authors' calculations.

Table 7.1. U.S. Growth Rate of Labor, Capital, and TFP

Below, we make assumptions about the future growth rates of these factors and use these estimates in forming a baseline forecast for future GDP. Before we proceed with our analysis, we summarize the average annual growth rates of these factors in *Table 7.1.*[51]

Our motivation in presenting this table is to find reasonable growth rates for future labor, capital, and TFP.

According to this table, the growth rates of labor, capital, and TFP in the 1990–2007 period were 1.28%, 2.74%, and 1.06%, respectively. These growth rates produce paths for future GDP, budget deficit, and debt that are very similar to the extended-baseline scenario projections of the CBO.[52] We will therefore assume that future growth rates of labor, capital, and TFP will be the same as their 1990–2007 values.

Equipped with these growth rates, we will then extend the values of labor, capital, and TFP into the future and use the production function to forecast future values of GDP. First, we present the future values of labor, capital, and TFP, and then we present our predicted values of GDP.

Source: Authors' calculations. See Chen, Imrohoroglu, and Imrohoroglu (2009).

Figure 7.5. Total Hours Worked

To show the labor input in *Figure 7.5*, we combined the time series paths for total hours worked in the United States between 1960 and 2010, with a projected path through 2021 under the assumption of a 1.28% growth.[53]

---

51 This is similar to Table 3.1 but summarizes growth rates for different time periods.

52 According to January 2011 CBO projections, the assumed growth rate of real GDP is 2.85% (CBO 2011a).

123

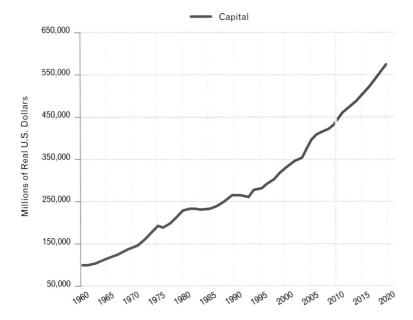

Figure 7.6. The Capital Stock

Our predictions for the future values of the U.S. capital stock are shown in *Figure 7.6*, which combines historical data for the capital stock with our projections until 2021. These projections also assume that the growth rate of capital will equal its average annual growth rate for the 1990–2007 period (2.74%).

Finally, our assumption on the growth rate of TFP is 1.06%, which is its average annualized growth rate between 1990 and 2007.

With these assumptions, the average deficit between 2012 and 2021 is projected to be 3.6%, which is the CBO projection under the extended-baseline scenario.

To illustrate the importance of assumptions about the future path of the inputs, consider the following case. The dramatic decline in total hours worked between 2007 and 2010 resulted in a much lower average growth rate for labor between 1990 and 2010 than between 1990 and 2007 (0.72% as opposed to 1.28% in *Table 7.1*). If we were to use the average growth rates of labor, capital, and TFP between 1990 and 2010 to project the growth rates into the future, the projected deficits between 2012 and 2021 would increase to 4.1% of GDP, as opposed to 3.6% of GDP.

However, a crucial component of the CBO projections is the assumption about the future path of the tax rates and the resulting tax revenues. As shown in *Figure 7.4*, revenues are projected to increase from 15% of GDP in 2010 to 21% in 2021 and to 31% in 2085 under the CBO's extended-baseline scenario.

One of the critical assumptions of this scenario is that the current law regarding the "alternative minimum tax" (AMT) will remain unchanged. Consequently, AMT is projected to affect a significant share of taxpayers over time, pushing up marginal and average tax rates.

Overall, the assumptions about current tax law result in marginal tax rates that increase from 25% in 2011 to 28% in 2012, to 29% in 2013, and to 35% in 2035.[54] These tax rates and tax revenues are without precedent. However, in calculating the resulting GDP and deficit projections, the CBO assumes no (or very small) behavioral responses by workers and business to the increases in tax rates. Given the current focus on how taxes impact the labor supply, it is important to consider an alternative scenario that incorporates a reasonable labor supply response.[55]

---

54 CBO (2011a).

55 Chen and Imrohoroglu (2012) calculate the debt-to-GDP ratio in 2035 to be 29% higher if labor supply responses are taken into consideration.

THE FISCAL CLIFF

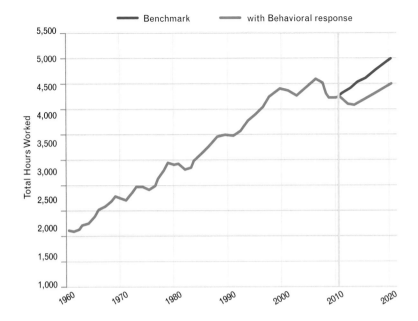

Figure 7.7. Total Hours Worked
(With and Without Behavioral Responses to Changes in Taxes)

Statistical estimates of labor supply elasticity range from 0.1 to over 1.0. However, most economists now converge on values of 0.25 to 0.5.[56]

In our alternative fiscal scenario, we assume that for a 10% increase in the tax rate (resulting in a 10% decrease in the after-tax wage rate), there will be a 2.5% decrease in employment and average hours worked. This assumption is equivalent to an elasticity of 0.25.

This is a very conservative estimate of the negative response of labor supply to the large increases in the tax rates projected by CBO. We think the private sector is quite rational and therefore will adjust to the new tax environment, resulting in a change in total hours worked. If we assume constant wages, and consider the proposed increases in tax rates assumed under the extended-baseline scenario as the starting point, employing our assumed labor supply elasticity of 0.25, we obtain projections for total hours worked, as displayed in *Figure 7.7*.

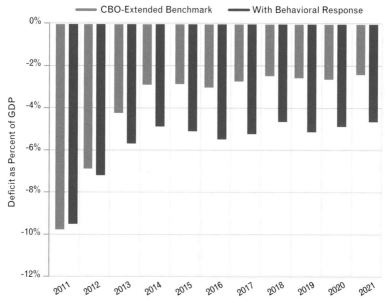

Source: Congressional Budget Office (2011a). Table 1-4, CBO's Baseline Projections, and authors' calculations.

Figure 7.8. Deficit Projections, 2011–2021

Assessing the impact of this alternative projection for the labor input on debt and deficit levels requires understanding its impact on capital stock and the GDP. In our projection, we have made appropriate adjustments to the capital input to keep the capital labor ratio growing at the same rate as in the benchmark case. The resulting projection for deficits is shown in *Figure 7.8*.

---

56 Chetty et al. (2011) argue an estimate of the short-run response of the labor supply on the extensive margin (employment) is 0.25, and that on the intensive margin (average hours worked) is 0.5. An elasticity of 0.5 would indicate a decline in the labor supply of 0.5% for a 1% decrease in the after-tax wage rate. Macroeconomists have used much higher elasticities, but in this study we follow the micro-labor literature and use the conservative elasticities.

127

According to these results, the sum of deficits between 2012 and 2021 is $6.971 trillion under the CBO projections with no behavioral response (that is, assuming no negative effects on labor supply), and $9.622 trillion with the conservative behavioral response discussed above.

This difference of $2.651 trillion is very large.

Remember the intense negotiations to extend the debt ceiling in the summer of 2011? That was to cut the deficit by only $2.1 trillion over 10 years.[57]

This simple calculation points out the need for a much larger fiscal response from policy makers if the economy is to return to any semblance of fiscal sustainability.

All we did was to alter the CBO projections with a very conservative behavioral response from the businesses and workers about how adversely they would be affected by the tax increases built into the CBO projections. We left other, more optimistic assumptions unchanged.

The result? An accumulated additional debt equal to 17.5% of GDP over the next decade, piling on top of the projected debt-to-GDP.

Under the extended-baseline scenario, debt-to-GDP in 2021 would now be 93.5%, and under CBO's alternative fiscal scenario, debt to GDP would climb to 118.5% in 2021.

This is above wartime levels of debt-to-GDP. Do we think the U.S. federal debt can climb that high without any negative consequences to the economy?

Of course not. In fact, well before debt reached such levels, our credit rating would likely suffer, and interest rates on U.S. Treasury bonds would increase.

Historically, one of the strengths of U.S. policy makers has been their foresight in dealing with potential crises early on. We have not seen this strength during America's ongoing fiscal debate—just the opposite.

57 CBO (2011c).

CHAPTER 8

THE LONG RUN

A quick snapshot of the federal government's 2012 fiscal year budget is worth repeating.

- Total spending: $3.796 trillion

- Total revenue: $2.469 trillion

- Budget deficit: $1.327 trillion

For a U.S. household with the median $50,000 of household income, this would mean spending 53.7% more than its income, or $76,873.

Without raising its income and curtailing its spending, this household is doomed. So is the U.S. federal government, which is another way of saying the U.S. taxpayer.

Of the $3.8 trillion of federal spending, the lion's share goes to Social Security at $773 billion, or 20.4% of the federal budget.

In addition, about 21% of the federal budget goes to health expenditures: Medicare, Medicaid, and the Children's Health Insurance Program.

In this chapter, we look at the economics and future of these two items, which make up 41% of the federal budget.

These two programs (public retirement and health spending) are the reasons why the CBO projects ongoing budget deficits no less than 4% of GDP year after year, piling onto the already high levels of government debt.

The burden on the budget (and taxpayers) of Social Security and health care expenditures will be exacerbated by increasingly unfavorable demographics. For that reason, we examine Social Security and Medicare expenditures in more detail below.

SOCIAL SECURITY

Social Security is the single largest federal government program. Of the 56 million beneficiaries in 2011, 81% were retired workers (or the survivors of deceased workers covered under the Old-Age and Survivors Insurance program) and 19% were disabled workers and their spouses and children (covered under the Disability Insurance program).

The financing of Social Security's $773 billion in fiscal year 2011[58] came primarily from payroll taxes, which burden employees and employers share. In 2011, the payroll tax rate on taxable income was 10.4%, up to a maximum of $106,800.[59]

SOCIAL SECURITY IN THEORY AND PRACTICE

In 2010, Social Security's outlays exceeded its revenues—a first since the Social Security Amendments of 1983. The Social Security Administration's board of trustees predicts that this gap will continue, with cash outlays exceeding revenues as the number of beneficiaries grows much faster than that of covered workers who pay into the system.

In the past, when revenues exceeded Social Security outlays, the proceeds were used by the federal government to finance other budget items, with special issue Treasury bonds used in lieu of the shortfall.

Since revenues will remain short of outlays, and increasingly so as the baby boomers start retiring in large numbers, the board of trustees projects that the trust fund will be exhausted in 2036. At that date, full benefits will not be able to be paid without either further increases in tax revenues or other reforms of the Social Security retirement program.

The main reason for Social Security's projected fiscal imbalance is the increasing size of the aging population. *Figure 8.1* shows that the old-age-dependency ratio—which is the fraction of the population age 65 or older relative to the percentage of the population ages 20–64—is expected to increase from 21% in 2000 to 36% by 2035.

58 CBO (2011a).
59 U.S. Department of the Treasury, Internal Revenue Service (2011c).

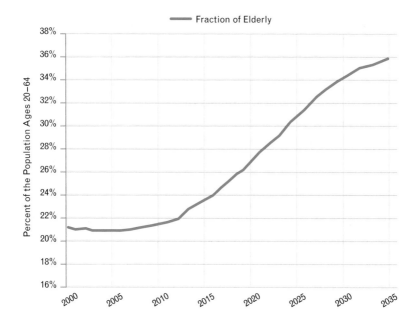

Figure 8.1. The Population Age 65 or Older
as a Percentage of the Population Ages 20 to 64

According to a 2010 Census Bureau report (Grayson and Velkoff, 2010) in 2050, the number of Americans age 65 and older is projected to be 88.5 million, which would be more than double its 2010 size.

As a result of these demographic changes, assets in the trust fund, which are actually special-issue Treasury bonds, will be exhausted by 2036. After this date, Social Security payroll tax revenues will cover only about three-quarters of promised benefits (75 cents for each dollar promised). Under both CBO scenarios, spending for the Social Security program is expected to rise from 4.8% of GDP in 2010 to above 6% of GDP by 2035.

Largely absent from the debate about Social Security's future viability has been a comprehensive evaluation of the unfunded— or "pay-as-you-go" (PAYGO)—nature of the U.S. Social Security system. Many countries are shifting away from a pure PAYGO system to a two-tiered version with a safety net plus private retirement accounts. The specific designs of these programs differ across countries; however, the impetus for these changes stems partly from some of the challenges that PAYGO systems face.

Currently, CBO projections acknowledge that Social Security taxes reduce the reward from work. The CBO assumes that the income and substitution effects of these changes will not be very different from each other and argues that the net effect of taxes will be little, if any, decline in the work effort.

As discussed in Chapter 2, the rationale for government intervention in private markets often comes from externalities or market failures. In this section, we highlight the main benefits and costs of social security in general, and the unfunded or PAYGO system in particular.

The main rationale for a government-provided pension system comes from the historic absence of markets for real annuities. Potential self-selection problems are often cited for the absence of these markets. In this case, a self-selection problem occurs if, for example, only individuals with a long life expectancy would choose to enter a contract that pays them an annuity (a pension) after retirement.

Thus, social security provides insurance for risks that are not easily insured in private markets. It can be thought of as a government-mandated rule that requires all individuals to enter such contracts and annuitize their accumulated assets in a personal retirement account, therefore eliminating the self-selection problem. Consequently, one of the potential benefits of social security is the annuity. If an individual lives longer than expected, an annuity that provides for old-age consumption later in life is welfare-enhancing. In other words, since the government provides old-age income, the individual will never run out of funds to spend on consumption.

Social security also serves as a commitment device for myopic individuals who otherwise may not save adequately for their old age.

In addition, social security distributes resources from high earners to low earners. The benefit formula that determines the "principal insurance amount" (PIA) is progressive. Relatively low lifetime income earners receive a higher fraction of their "average indexed monthly income" (AIME) as PIA. Higher earners receive a much lower fraction of their average income as retirement benefits.

Finally, an unfunded social security system may also improve the intergenerational allocation of risk. If there is substantial generation-specific income risk due to phenomena such as the Great Depression or a significant stock market downturn, fiscal policy tools like public debt or unfunded social security might be used to spread this systemic risk across many generations.

At the same time, there are certain inefficiencies or social costs associated with a PAYGO system.

First, unfunded social security discourages private saving. Young workers with high marginal propensities to save are taxed, and those resources are given to retirees with low marginal propensities to save. Thus, those with the higher propensity to save have less money to save due to social security taxes. Consequently, total savings and the capital stock will be lower under an unfunded social security system than a funded system. This means a smaller supply of loanable funds that could go to financing businesses and helping to create new jobs.

Second, unfunded systems discourage work effort, since the payroll tax paid by the worker has less than perfect linkage, if any, with the retirement benefit that the worker will receive. Thus, the labor supply in the economy is adversely affected, as job creation is curtailed and market work is penalized.

Third, they distort the retirement decision and encourage early retirement. This clearly reduces the labor supply of older and experienced workers.

Economic research that carefully examines these benefits and costs typically finds that without significant aggregate risks, such as a sharp decline in the stock market, the negative impact of a PAYGO social security system outweighs its benefits.

There are two important and valid concerns over making wholesale changes in our current Social Security system.

First, privatizing Social Security exposes old-age consumption to systemic risks, which can be significant if private retirement funds lose significant value around the time individuals are close to retirement age. A large fraction of retirees rely on Social Security as the main source of their old-age income, and if these incomes plunge because of stock market losses, there will be pressure on government to cover some or all of the losses.

Second, there would be significant transitional costs associated with moving to another system, which would be difficult to deal with, especially in the current economic (and political) environment.

In addition, Social Security is not the most urgent fiscal challenge facing the United States. Even if no changes are made to the current system, a majority of the benefits will still be financed by unchanged payroll taxes in years to come. However, with the projected shortfall of 25% of benefits, large sums of new taxes must be raised to maintain benefits at current levels.

As a result, Social Security reform also needs to be a part of fiscal policy discussions today. We believe that relatively small and reasonable fixes can restore fiscal sustainability to the U.S. public pension system without major surgery. For example, De Nardi, İmrohoroğlu, and Sargent (1999) consider a menu of Social Security reform, taking into account the transitional costs, and find that extending the normal retirement age by two years goes a long way in mitigating the projected fiscal burden of the aging on the economy.

In addition, recent research by İmrohoroğlu and Sagiri (2011) suggest that postponing the normal retirement age by two years, together with extending the early retirement age by two years, would minimize the future shortfall in the Social Security system. The main reasons for this improvement is (a) the increase in the labor supply of individuals that results in response to a smaller payroll tax to finance the system and (b) the increase in private saving, which is induced by a longer work life.

These changes in our retirement program would make it possible to maintain Social Security as we know it today. This is especially important if the Social Security reform is to be consistent with preserving what works for a large part of the society in a way that also promotes long-run growth.

SOCIAL SECURITY IN THE FUTURE

How do we go forward in restoring fiscal health to Social Security?

Among the three major proposals on Social Security, the key component is to gradually raise the early and normal retirement ages to reach 64 and 69, respectively, by 2075.

As a large body of economic research indicates, this change alone would provide most of what would be needed to bring the budget of the Social Security Administration into balance.

Second, the payroll tax base would be raised to generate more revenue from higher income earners, and at the same time, the benefit formula would be changed to lower the benefits of high earners and raise those of the oldest and poorest beneficiaries. This would enhance the social insurance role of Social Security. There is support for this idea from an economic point of view.

Third, new state and local government employees would be directed to the mandatory Social Security program, providing much-needed revenues in the short term and relieving state and local governments from eventual bankruptcy due to the unfunded nature of huge defined benefits programs.

For example, the California Public Employees' Retirement System (CalPERS) is the largest state pension program, and it has a large unfunded liability. Assessments of the size of this shortfall depend on various assumptions but can be as high as $500 billion.

The main reason why these public state retirement systems are in trouble is that the contribution rates of their employees depend on expected future returns from the public fund. For private corporations, federal law requires that the expected future return on a fund be based on investing in lower-yielding but safer assets such as bonds. This practice produces an estimate of 5–6%.

CalPERS, on the other hand, currently uses an estimate of 7.5% future return to determine the current contribution rate of state public employees. In the next few years, when the actual return on the state pension fund is less than 7.5% a year on average, guess who will pick up the tab? California taxpayers.

Shifting from this state-taxpayer-financed defined benefit retirement system, which is unsustainable, to a better-designed federal social security system would not only help raise the revenue for Social Security but it would also lower the burden on state coffers.[60]

HEALTH CARE

How large is health care expenditure in the United States altogether? How does it compare with expenditures in other advanced economies? What is the future of these expenditures? Are there any parts of our health expenditure system that we can reform to help restore fiscal sustainability?

In this chapter, we describe the issues surrounding our health expenditures, predictions over the next few decades, and aspects of the system that should be fixed to obtain future fiscal balance in the economy.

In 2009, total spending on health care in the United States was about $2.3 trillion,[61] with Medicare accounting for $502.3 billion and Medicaid $373.9 billion.

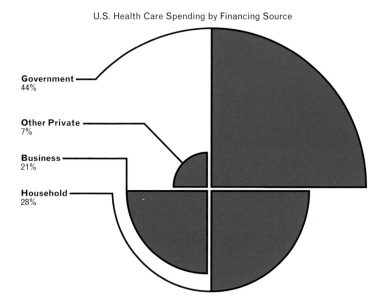

U.S. Health Care Spending by Financing Source

Government
44%

Other Private
7%

Business
21%

Household
28%

Source: Centers for Medicare & Medicaid Services, U.S. Department of Health & Human Services (2009).

Figure 8.2. U.S. Health Care by Financing Source

Of this total spending, 44% was financed by public sources (i.e., government), with the remainder coming from private sources. *Figure 8.2* shows the breakdown of financing of national health care spending by source. Spending financed by businesses, households, and other private sponsors was 21%, 28%, and 7%, respectively.

According to CBO estimates, 39% of the insured population is covered by either Medicaid or Medicare.

60 It is worth mentioning here that the president's 2010 National Commission on Fiscal Responsibility and Reform provided an actionable blueprint for reforming our public pension system.

61 Total spending refers to total national spending, not just spending by government.

More specifically, the CBO estimates that in 2010, 150 million people under the age of 65 were receiving health insurance through an employment-based health plan, 13 million bought insurance directly from an insurer, 48 million were covered by Medicare, 56 million were covered by Medicaid, and 50 million were uninsured.[62]

Public expenditures on health care have exploded over the past few decades. *Figure 8.3* displays this dramatic increase in U.S. expenditures on Medicare and Medicaid since 1970 as a percentage of GDP.[63]

According to the projections under the alternative fiscal scenario provided by the CBO, these expenditures are expected to rise to 6.9% in 2020, to 9.2% in 2030, and to 11.4% in 2040, and continue rising.

Consequently, this category of government expenditures is the most significant and alarming one for future projections.

Without the substantial tax increases assumed under the alternative fiscal scenario, this level of spending on health care contributes to a projected deficit of 6.6% of GDP, excluding net interest (15.5% including net interest), and federal debt held by the public totaling 187% of GDP in 2035.

Moreover, under the alternative fiscal scenario, the deficit by 2085 is projected to increase to 14.5% of GDP, excluding net interest.

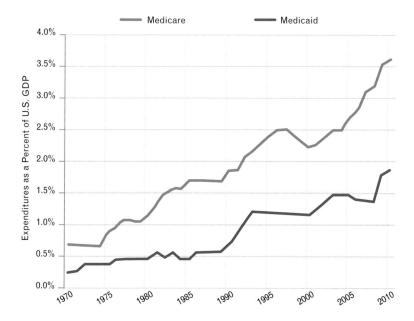

Source: Congressional Budget Office (2011c). Figure B-1.

Figure 8.3. U.S. Medicare and Medicaid Expenditures as a Percentage of GDP

Controlling health care costs is vital for the future fiscal stability of the United States. Otherwise, medical expenditures could be taking twice as much of our income by 2040, leaving less to spend on housing, education, and other critical expenditures.

While this point is well accepted by academicians and policy makers, the rise in health care costs is a complicated issue that is not confined to the discussion of the expenditures borne by the government.

62 CBO (2011a).

63 CBO (2011a).

The factors behind rising health care costs have sparked substantial research in economics, some of which we summarize below.

It will be useful to separate health care costs into two issues.

The first issue is the long-term growth of health expenditures in both the United States and other OECD countries. Between 1960 and 2009, health care expenditures as a percentage of GDP increased from 5.1% to 17.4% in the United States. What are the major causes behind this increase?

The second issue is related to the differences in health care cost between the United States and its peer countries. Why are health care costs in the United States higher than those in the peer countries? What drives these differences?

LONG-RUN TRENDS IN HEALTH EXPENDITURES

In the United States, expenditures on health care have outpaced growth in the economy for several decades, accounting for an increasingly large share of the country's GDP.

However, the disproportionate rise in health care costs over this time period is not unique to the United States. Several OECD countries with very different health care systems have also experienced increases over time. *Figure 8.4* plots the ratio of health care expenditures to GDP in developed countries between 1960 and 2009. This figure shows that while U.S. health care expenditures more than tripled from 1960 to 2009, Spain experienced a more than sixfold increase over the same time period.

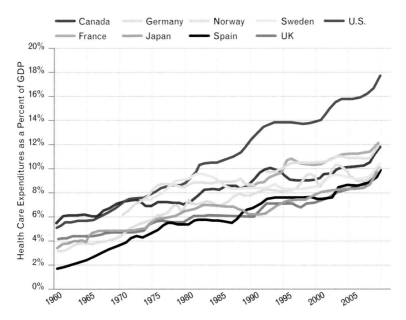

Source: OECD (2011b), last updated July 21, 2011.

Figure 8.4. Health Care Expenditures as a Percentage of GDP, 1960–2009

The average annual growth rate of health care expenditures between 1970 and 2009 was 2.5% in the United States, 1.5% in Canada, 2.3% in France, 1.7% in Germany, 2.2% in Japan, 2.5% in Norway, 3.8% in Spain, 1% in Sweden, and 1.9% in the United Kingdom.

While health care expenditures have been increasing significantly in many countries since the 1960s, what is even more striking is how much more the U.S. spends on health care as a percentage of GDP than other developed countries.

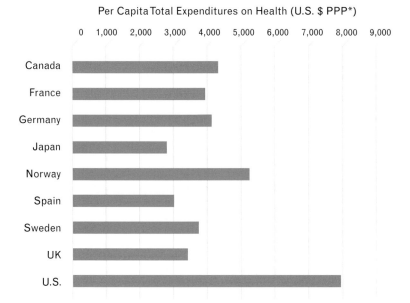

Per Capita Total Expenditures on Health (U.S. $ PPP*)

Source: OECD (2011b), last updated July 21, 2011.
* Purchasing power parity (PPP)

Figure 8.5. Health Care Expenditures per Capita, 2009.

In 2009, U.S. spending on health care was about 17% of GDP, while spending in these eight other developed countries was 9–12% of GDP. *Figure 8.5* displays total health care expenditures per capita in the same set of countries in 2009.[64]

While U.S. expenditures per person were about $8,000, the average of the rest of the countries presented in this figure was about $3,000.

Just how much of this rising health care cost is borne by the government? *Figure 8.6* displays the fraction of health care expenditures that is paid by public sources (i.e., government sources). As *Figure 8.6* shows, the part of health care expenditures paid by the government is significantly lower in the United States (about 50%) than in its peer countries (70–84%).

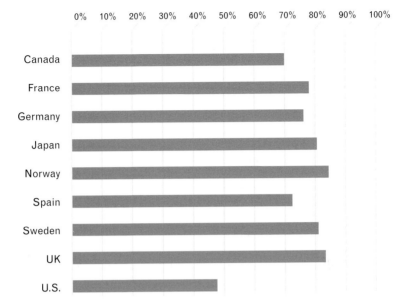

Source: OECD (2011b), last updated July 21, 2011.

Figure 8.6. Public Expenditures as a Percentage of
Total Health Expenditures, 2009

Thus, while health care costs are higher as a percentage of GDP in the United States than in other countries, the U.S. government bears a smaller share of those higher costs than governments in other developed countries.

To adjust these spending levels for differences in the sizes of the underlying populations, we present the average public health care expenditures on a per capita basis between 1960 and 2009 in *Figure 8.7*. This figure shows that, after normalizing public spending to account for population size, there is less of a difference between health care spending in the United States and that in other countries.

64 Expenditures are in PPP-adjusted dollars.

147

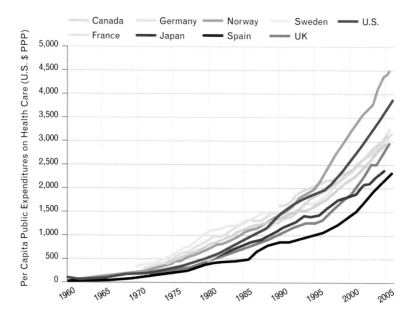

Source: OECD (2011b), last updated July 21, 2011.

Figure 8.7. Average Public Health Care Expenditures per Capita,
1960–2009

Nonetheless, public expenditures on health care per person are still greater in the United States than in all other countries in the sample, except Norway. In 2009, these expenditures borne by governments ranged from highs of $4,500 per person in Norway and $3,794 in the United States to a low of $2,258 in Spain.

So why are health care costs increasing faster than GDP? Some factors that may explain the disproportionate increase include the following:

- Increases in the size of the elderly population

- Increases in insurance coverage

- Decreases in coinsurance rates

- Supplier-induced (i.e., physician-induced) demand

- Increases in income per capita, under the hypothesis that health care is a luxury good

- Better medical technology

In the next section, we summarize some of the main findings from this research to help better understand why health care costs have increased so dramatically over the past 50 years.

FACTORS DRIVING HIGHER HEALTH CARE SPENDING IN THE U.S.

Some economic studies seek to identify and quantify the factors that may explain the increase in U.S. health care spending. Newhouse (1992) considers several factors. Among them is the impact of the increase in the size of the elderly population[65] on health care expenditures. His results indicate that the increase in the relative size of the elderly population from 8% of the

---

65 The fraction of the total population that is over age 65.

population in 1950 to 12% in 1987 accounts for only 15% of the increase in total spending. This is far below the actual increase in expenditures per capita that took place over this period.

Another possible cause of the higher levels of health care spending is supplier-induced demand, whereby physicians generate more demand for their services if patients are relatively uninformed consumers. While this may play some role in overall costs, it seems unlikely to explain the substantial rise over time, because consumers are becoming increasingly sophisticated. Overall, Newhouse (1992) concludes that the invention of new and expensive medical technologies has caused health spending to rise over time.

Some economists have argued that the observed increase in health care spending could be a rational response to the increase in personal income. This line of research asserts that if health spending is a superior good, then as people get wealthier, they will devote a larger share of their income to spending on it. Various measures of the benefits of this higher spending, such as gains associated with increased life expectancy and improved medical technology, find that these benefits may actually exceed the increase in health care costs.

Suen (2006) also argues that all of the rise in medical expenditures since the 1950s and 60% of the increase in life expectancy can be explained by the increase in income and improvements in medical technology.

Lawver (2010) estimates that the quality of medical goods and services at the aggregate level has increased by 2.2% per year between 1996 and 2007. But this finding implies that the relative price of medical goods and services has declined by 0.5% per year over this time period, instead of increasing by 1.6% per year, as U.S. Bureau of Labor Statistics estimates suggest.

In addition, Hall and Jones (2007) show that the value of longevity gains that took place after the 1950s easily justifies the rise in health spending from 5.2% of GDP in 1950 to 15.4% in 2000, as life expectancy increased from 68.2 years in 1950 to 76.9 years in 2000. Similarly, Murphy and Topel (2006) argue that the value of the improved life expectancy between 1970 and 2000 was $95 trillion—about three times larger than medical spending over this period. In other studies, researchers suggest that improvements in cardiovascular health and in the survival of premature infants in the U.S. health care system have been worth their high expenditures.[66]

However, when assessing the value of medical technology, one must recognize that many other factors may have played a role in increased longevity. Changes such as better nutrition, exercise, sanitation, and smoking cessation, as well as improvement in medical care, have contributed to the changes in longevity. These considerations make it difficult to assess the productivity of medical care or to conduct a cost-benefit analysis of medical care.

Overall, some of this research indicates that the increase in medical expenditures experienced in the United States may not necessarily be a cause for concern.

If these considerations are valid, then the increase in public expenditures in health care appears less surprising. They would simply be following the general trends in health care.

---

66 See, for example, Cutler (2004) and Murphy and Topel (2006).

DIFFERENCES IN HEALTH CARE EXPENDITURES BETWEEN THE U.S. AND PEER COUNTRIES

Why are health care expenditures in the United States so much higher as a percentage of GDP than in other developed countries? Can some of the factors identified previously as possible determinants of rising health care costs provide any insights into the answer to this question?

For example, do the demographics, such as the fraction of the population that is elderly, or the higher level of wealth explain why the United States spends more on health care than other developed countries?

Is the standard of care in the United States superior to that of other health care systems?

Or is it that certain inefficiencies within the U.S. system explain the higher observed cost?

How much of the relatively high U.S. health care spending is due to the costs of administration, physicians, and pharmaceuticals?

We explore these questions in this section.

Our main finding is that demographics and quality differences do not account for the higher cost of health care in the United States.

Rather, higher spending is driven by higher costs of hospital administration and physician care, the disconnect between prices and demand (due to the nature of the third-party payer system), and the absence of cost-benefit analyses for prescribed treatments.

WEALTH AND DEMOGRAPHICS

As discussed earlier, there is evidence that the richer the country, the more is spent on health care. For example, Reinhardt, Hussey, and Anderson (2002) found that, on average, an increase in GDP per capita of $10,000 is estimated to increase per capita health spending by $966. Their estimates suggest, however, that the United States has spent $1,300 more per capita on health care than would have been predicted by its higher GDP alone than other OECD countries.

It also appears unlikely that the high U.S. health care costs are a function of the size of the aging population. *Table 8.1*, which is from Reinhardt, Hussey, and Anderson (2002), shows that many countries with a larger elderly population have lower per capita expenditures. In 1999, the elderly population (age 65 or older) in France was 15.9% of the population and health care expenditures per capita were $2,115, compared with the United States, where the elderly population was only 12.3% of the population, but the spending on health care was $4,358 per capita—106% higher than in France.

Health spending, population age, and health employment
in 30 OECD countries. Selected years: 1990-1999

	Health Spending per Capita ($ PPP)		Real Annual Growth in Health Spending per Capita (national currency units at 1995 GDP prices)		
	1990	1999	1970-1980	1980-1990	1990-1999
Australia	1,682	2,085	-	2.7%	3.7%
Austria	1,538	2,014	7.4	1.4	3.2
Belgium	1,592	2,181	8.1	3.4	3.5
Canada	2,142	2,463	3.0	4.0	1.7
Czech Republic	735	983	-	-	4.1
Denmark	1,855	2,275	-	0.8	1.8
Finland	1,649	1,547	4.5	4.8	-0.2
France	1,940	2,115	5.4	3.6	2.1
Germany	2,045	2,361	6.1	2.1	1.8
Greece	902	1,198	5.4	2.6	2.7
Hungary	652	762	-	-	1.6
Iceland	1,756	2,287	7.6	4.2	2.5
Ireland	1,016	1,534	8.5	1.1	5.6
Italy	1,681	1,832	6.3	3.6	1.1
Japan	1,381	1,796	7.0	2.7	3.7
Korea	474	868	-	-	6.2
Luxembourg	1,897	2,543	7.2	4.3	4.2
Mexico	332	419	-	-	3.5
Netherlands	1,791	2,259	-	2.2	2.4
New Zealand	1,196	1,505	2.0	2.7	2.9
Norway	1,740	2,388	9.1	3.1	3.8
Poland	329	535	-	-	5.3
Portugal	784	1,203	11.5	4.1	5.2
Slovakia	-	668	-	-	-
Spain	1,040	1,189	6.9	4.7	2.7
Sweden	1,904	1,732	4.4	1.0	-0.1
Switzerland	2,275	2,853	4.2	2.8	2.7
Turkey	218	316	-	3.6	6.1
UK	1,236	1,569	4.1	3.1	3.3
U.S.	3,495	4,358	4.4	5.5	3.0
Median	**1,592**	**1,764**	**6.2**	**3.1**	**3.0**

Source: Reinhardt, Hussey, and Anderson (2002).

Table 8.1. Health Spending and Demographics in 30 OECD Countries

154

Percent of GDP Spent on Health	Percent of Population Age 65 or Older	Total Health Employment per 1,000	
1999	1999	1999	
8.6	12.2	31.2	Australia
8.2	15.5	-	Austria
8.8	16.8	21.1	Belgium
9.3	12.4	25.2	Canada
7.4	13.8	21.6	Czech Republic
8.4	14.9	26.2	Denmark
6.8	14.8	46.7	Finland
9.3	15.9	26.4	France
10.3	16.8	42.3	Germany
8.4	17.0	11.8	Greece
6.8	14.6	16.1	Hungary
8.7	11.6	33.6	Iceland
6.8	11.3	19.8	Ireland
7.9	17.6	19.1	Italy
7.5	16.7	21.2	Japan
5.4	6.8	-	Korea
6.1	14.3	13.0	Luxembourg
5.3	5.3	6.7	Mexico
8.7	13.6	23.8	Netherlands
8.1	11.7	-	New Zealand
8.5	15.4	71.4	Norway
6.2	12.0	-	Poland
7.7	15.1	13.1	Portugal
6.3	11.3	-	Slovakia
7.0	16.6	15.7	Spain
7.9	17.8	35.3	Sweden
10.4	15.2	53.7	Switzerland
4.8	5.3	3.3	Turkey
6.9	15.7	29.9	UK
12.9	12.3	32.6	U.S.
7.9	**14.7**	**23.8**	**Median**

Table 8.1. Health Spending and Demographics in 30 OECD Countries

155

QUALITY OF HEALTH CARE

Is the U.S. health care system more costly because it provides for a higher quality of care than the health care systems in other countries?

This is a difficult question to answer because observed differences may be due to factors unrelated to heath care systems, such as behavioral, genetic, and other factors.

There are several comparisons that researchers have conducted. For example, in terms of aggregate outcomes, such as life expectancy or infant mortality, studies suggest that the United States lags behind many other OECD countries. In addition, the U.S. system is much less accessible, with more that 40 million uninsured Americans.

On the other hand, parts of the U.S. system are high-quality, including the availability of cutting-edge drugs and early-stage treatments. And wait times to see a physician, especially a specialist, tend to be lower in the United States than in many other OECD countries.

Overall, however, it is difficult to conclude that the higher U.S. health care expenditures can be easily explained by higher quality. It is possible that the United States has a less efficient health care production technology, since similar health outcomes are observed for much lower spending.

COST OF INPUTS

In order to further understand the differences in health care costs, we can examine the differences in the costs of inputs. There is some indication that the inputs that go into the production of health care are more expensive in the United States than in other wealthy countries.

In terms of the share of GDP spent on pharmaceuticals, a 2008 report by the global consulting firm McKinsey indicates that in 2006, the United States spent 35% more than Canada and almost twice the OECD average. Between 2003 and 2006, spending on drugs grew at 6.9% per year. The McKinsey report concluded that this higher spending on drugs was mostly due to higher prices, not to higher dosages or higher branded drug consumption.

Some have suggested that the prices of pharmaceuticals in the United States are subsidizing pharmaceutical R&D for the rest of the world, or that the relatively high income in the United States is driving up pharmaceutical prices. But these and other explanations fail to account for the differences in pharmaceutical costs across the United States and the OECD countries.

There is some evidence that administrative costs may explain, in part, why spending on health care is higher in the United States (relative to GDP) than in other developed countries.

Spending on health administration and insurance in the United States was twice as high as that in France—the second-highest spender—and almost five times the OECD average in 1999. Woolhandler, Campbell, and Himmelstein (2003) estimate that administrative costs comprise 31% of health care spending in the United States compared with 16% in Canada. They estimate that in 1999 the U.S. system consumed $1,059 per person in administrative costs, compared with just $307 in Canada.

In addition, there is some evidence that spending on physicians is higher in the United States than in peer countries. Despite the fact that the United States has fewer physicians per 1,000 people than the OECD median, total U.S. spending on physicians as a percentage of GDP is double the OECD median.[67]

The 2008 McKinsey report on health care also reports that in 2006, U.S. general practitioners made 4.1 times per capita GDP, compared with 2.8 times per capita GDP in other OECD countries. Specialists made 6.5 times per capita GDP in the United States, while the OECD average was 3.9. According to its estimates, higher earnings of U.S. physicians add $64 billion in costs to the U.S. health care system, which is a $2 trillion industry.

There are some difficulties in making cross-country comparisons of physicians' salaries, due to differences in data collection methods and the reporting years. Nevertheless, the data displayed in *Figures 8.8* and *8.9*, showing average remunerations of specialists and general practitioners in a group of countries, respectively, display marked differences between the United States and the rest of the countries.[68] In 2007, average remuneration for general practitioners in the United States was around $170,000. The country with the next highest general practitioner salaries was Denmark, at around $110,000. Similarly, remuneration for specialists was about $211,000 in the United States, compared with $126,000 for the next highest country, the Netherlands. Factors such as the high cost of U.S. medical education are unlikely to account for all the differences in payments received by physicians.

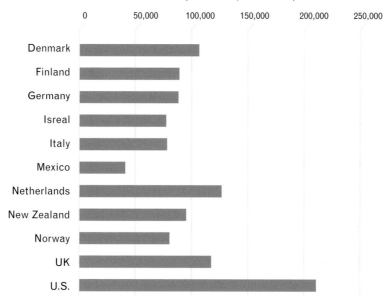

Remuneration of Specialists (U.S. $ PPP)

Source: OECD (2011a). Data extracted September 6, 2011.

Figure 8.8. Remuneration of Specialists, 2007

---

67 Reinhardt, Hussey, and Anderson (2002).
68 Data from authors' calculations and OECD.StatExtracts (2011a).

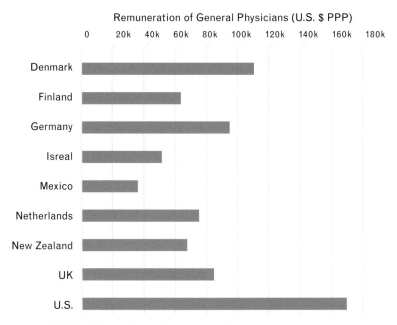

Remuneration of General Physicians (U.S. $ PPP)

Source: OECD.StatExtracts (2011a). Data extracted September 6, 2011.

Figure 8.9. Average Remuneration of General Physicians, 2007

The McKinsey report concludes that hospital administration and physician care account for almost 85% of the excess U.S. spending (above what is expected given high U.S. income levels), compared with the other OECD countries. However, this observation does not explain the reasons behind these higher costs.

STRUCTURE OF THE HEALTH CARE SYSTEM

A possible cause of higher U.S. health care spending may be related to a number of inefficiencies in the health care system:

- Malpractice litigation

- Cost shifting (providers charging higher prices to privately insured patients to offset their losses from uncompensated care)

- Lack of attention to price or cost effectiveness, due to the third-party payment system, and substitution of more costly interventions with no cost-benefit analysis

We explore each of these possible inefficiency explanations and find that the third-party payment system, which results in a lack of sensitivity to prices and costs, is likely to account for a significant share of the high U.S. health care costs.

- Malpractice: While malpractice litigation imposes costs, the direct expenditures seem to account for a small fraction of total expenditures.[69] However, there is also a potentially important indirect cost of this channel. Fear of malpractice suits may make physicians engage in defensive medicine, where they are likely to order more diagnostics tests than necessary. Using data on all elderly Medicare beneficiaries treated for serious heart disease in 1984, 1987, and 1990, Kessler and McClellan (1996) report that "malpractice reforms that directly reduce provider liability pressure lead to reductions of 5 to 9% in medical expenditures without substantial effects on mortality or medical complications."

---

69 According to the 2008 McKinsey report, the total direct cost of malpractice suits in 2006 was $30.3 billion.

161

• Cost Shifting: Another potentially important channel for high health care costs is the possibility that health care providers are charging higher prices to privately insured patients to offset their losses from uncompensated care. Hadley, Holahan, Coughlin and Miller (2008) estimate the magnitude of total uncompensated care (i.e., care not paid for by the uninsured or health insurance) as $54.3 billion in 2008. However, they show that payments from different public and private sources during this time covered 75% of these expenses. They estimate that about $14.1 billion could be financed by cost shifting, which represents about 1.7 % of private health insurance costs. Thus, these results suggest cost shifting is unlikely to play a major role in the high U.S. health care costs.

• Third-Party Payment System: One feature of the health care system that is unique to the U.S. is the tax deductibility of employer-provided health insurance. This system leads to significant inefficiencies in the portability and continuity of health insurance. Cogan, Hubbard, and Kessler (2011) argue that the third-party payment system makes buying health care through insurance (instead of out of pocket) look less expensive to the worker than it really is and makes people less sensitive to price considerations when consuming health care. They argue that abolishing the tax deductibility alone would reduce health care costs by 6.2%.

Garber (2008) comments, "For the well-insured, obtaining health care in the United States is like dining in a sumptuous restaurant that has menus without prices. A price-free menu encourages diners to ignore cost when making their selections."

The 2008 McKinsey report also discusses the lack of transparency of prices in the U.S. health care system, saying that it is unique when compared with other health systems. Currently, there are very limited options for comparison shopping by price in the United States. Most consumers are fairly insensitive to price, since they pay only a small fraction of their costs out of pocket, and typically know only the price they pay, not the ultimate price charged to the insurer.

In addition, the third-party payment system of health insurance is likely to play a significant role in why technological improvements in this sector do not result in price declines (as they have in other industries, such as computers or automobiles). Neither the ultimate consumer nor the service provider is motivated to reduce costs.

In the United States, there are weak incentives for health care providers or hospitals to seek out cost-effective treatments.[70] The fee-for-service reimbursement method, which is widely used in health care, creates strong incentives for health care providers to seek out more expensive treatment options. Weinstein and Skinner (2010) argue for the importance of an assessment of the added improvement in health outcomes relative to cost, such as cost-effectiveness analysis, which is used by many European countries. This analysis shows that the range of incremental cost per quality-adjusted life year gained for different procedures is stunningly large. Put differently, we are paying a huge amount to extend life a little bit, after adjusting for the quality of life.

For example, annual screening for cervical cancer costs about $800,000 more for every life year gained than biennial screening costs. Overall, Weinstein and Skinner argue that the substitution of more costly interventions and the introduction of expensive new diagnostic tests, procedures, and other treatments have added significantly to heath care costs.

---

70 While insurers representing large numbers of the insured are able to bargain for lower prices, ultimately consolidation of many hospitals has enabled them to secure higher prices (CBO 2008, Chapter 5).

WHAT ARE THE OPTIONS GOING FORWARD?

If left alone, U.S. public spending on health care will continue to increase at a rate similar to the increase in overall health care costs. Medicare and Medicaid made up about 6% of GDP in 2010. After 2030, this will be about 10% of GDP. Baicker and Skinner (2011) predict that the top marginal tax rates may have to rise by 70% to pay for the expected increases in these programs. The efficiency loss due to higher taxes, in this case, results in 5–11% declines in output by 2060.

It is important to address the inefficiencies in the overall health care system in order to satisfactorily address the increasing government spending on health care.

There are few different approaches the United States can take to curb rising health care costs.

The first approach would involve imposing explicit or implicit rationing on the use of health care services paid for by the government. For example, as of this writing, California is considering the possibility of imposing a cap on how often people with Medicaid can go to the doctor.

Another option would be to create institutes that would have the authority to make official determinations of the clinical effectiveness and cost-effectiveness of medical treatments, procedures, drugs, and devices.

The other alternative is to devise changes that would increase the price sensitivity of consumers and provide information to customers that will help them in making choices for themselves.

Currently, there are many different proposals for reforming the health care system. One of them is from economists John F. Cogan, R. Glenn Hubbard, and Daniel P. Kessler (2006).

They propose several major changes:

• Allow all individuals to deduct expenditures on health care (on insurance and out-of-pocket) as long as they purchase insurance that covers at least catastrophic expenditures. This change will make insurance more affordable for those who are unable to obtain insurance through their employers. There will be increased incentives to purchase health plans with lower premiums and higher copayments, and consumers will also become more cost-conscious. These changes will have two effects. First, since out-of-pocket expenditures will become tax-deductible, there will be an increase in health care expenditures. At the same time, it will be in consumers' financial interest to choose health care plans with higher deductibles, which will lower health care costs. The authors show, using reasonable assumptions, that the second effect will prevail and overall health care spending will go down. This policy will also increase incentives for the uninsured to purchase health insurance and increase the fairness of the federal tax system. The proposal also includes tax credits for low-income households that would subsidize 25% of health expenses.

• Create a nationwide health insurance market that would function alongside the state-regulated insurance market. Currently, each U.S. state specifies the rules by which its insurance markets operate. Consequently, there are significant differences across states with respect to prices, as well as covered benefits. The authors argue that state-mandated benefits and rate regulations have driven up health care costs. Individuals and employers should instead be free to choose from alternative plans. This approach would also increase the portability of health insurance and lower a potential barrier to relocation.

The authors also propose a subsidy for the chronically ill, since competitive markets for insurance may not work well for this segment of the population. Adverse selection is important when a patient's high expenditures are predictable in advance. So for these cases, instead of creating regulations that will have other, unintended consequences, they propose subsidizing the chronically ill. Providing insurance for catastrophic illnesses, on the other hand, would not be subsidized, since for such cases insurance markets are designed to work well.

• Expand access to health information through better use of report cards and clinical practice guidelines. The suggestions include better availability of data that would facilitate a privately produced portfolio of different types of report cards and help by the surgeon general to make accessible guidelines and generally recommended treatments.

• Control anticompetitive behavior. Curtailing the power of the Accreditation Council for Graduate Medical Education will be among the first steps in this direction. The authors cite evidence that areas with high concentration of market power by hospitals suffer higher costs and lower quality in health care services.

• Reform the malpractice system. States without reasonable limits on noneconomic damages in medical malpractice lawsuits experience lower physician availability and higher health care costs. In addition, physicians engage in more defensive medicine.

THE FISCAL CLIFF

CHAPTER 9

"IF NOT US, WHO? IF NOT NOW, WHEN?"

The U.S. government needs substantial budget reform to restore fiscal balance, reduce uncertainty for businesses and households, and make our tax policy more efficient and fair.

This book's historical data and future projections (of government expenditures and revenue) have shown that deficits and debt will increase to unprecedented levels unless Congress moves swiftly. Posturing, dithering, and kicking the can farther down the road bleed the U.S. economy month by month, year by year, and soon enough, decade by decade.

A good example of how the current economy looks different from past economies can be seen in *Figure 9.1*, which compares changes in U.S employment across different recessions. The decline in employment that we have experienced in this recession is worse than the harshest recession in the U.S. since the Great Depression.

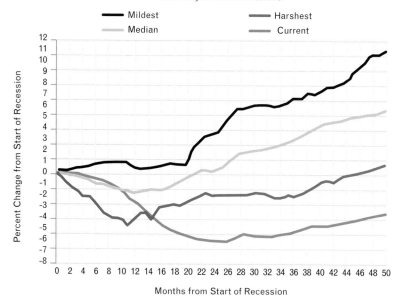

Source: Federal Reserve Bank of Minneapolis.

Figure 9.1. Recessions and Employment

Moreover, more than four years after the start of this recession, employment remains very low. While there are likely to be several reasons for anemic job growth, future projections on debt and possible increases in tax rates must be playing a role in businesses' decisions. How could they not?

However, if policy makers try to resolve America's fiscal problems primarily by raising tax revenues, there will likely be negative consequences. Higher tax rates mean fewer jobs created—and this decline in labor supply will result in a reduced GDP.

While the exact magnitude of these consequences may be disputed, when the CBO allows for the negative effects of higher tax rates, its GDP projections decline 1–3% by 2021, and 6.7–17.6% by 2035.

A reduction of nearly 18% by 2035 is another way of saying our income (or living standard) will fall by 18% in 2035.

That is not progress; it is regress.

On the other hand, if policy makers try to resolve the nation's fiscal problems primarily by cutting expenditures, then careful attention must be paid to how much can actually be accomplished. Concentrating only on discretionary spending will plainly not suffice.

Furthermore, this book has also shown that health care expenditures will significantly increase in the future. If polices to curb the deficit leave health care intact, then discretionary spending (education and defense) must undergo major cuts.

To prevent a "redline" debt-to-GDP ratio of over 100%, the U.S. government must promptly implement a comprehensive and rigorous two-pronged attack:

- Fundamental Tax Reform

    - Increase tax revenue by eliminating deductions (mortgage interest, health insurance premiums, charitable giving, etc.) that favor certain industries over others (without economic rationale). This will raise the average tax rates while creating greater labor supply.

    - Reduce marginal tax rates; this promotes job creation and economic growth.

• Fundamental Reform of the Entitlement Programs

   • Reduce the growth of health care expenditures—the projected increase in public medical expenditures is the single largest fiscal burden on the U.S.

   • Increase the early and normal retirement ages to match the increase in longevity; raise the benefits of poorer retirees and lower those of wealthier retirees; and incentivize private saving for retirement.

Which brings us back to where we started—there is a comprehensive and rigorous budget plan that addresses these issues.

Deficit Reduction Under Simpson-Bowles Proposal (In Billions)

	2012	2013	2014	2015	2016	2017
Discretionary Spending	$49	$102	$141	$172	$194	$215
Mandatory Spending	$1	$32	$47	$54	$64	$70
Spending in the Tax Code/ Tax Reform	$0	$20	$40	$80	$90	$105
Other Revenue	$1	$5	$11	$18	$27	$32
Net Interest Savings	$1	$5	$16	$33	$58	$87
Total Deficit Reduction*	$52	$164	$255	$357	$433	$509
Projected Deficit Under Plan (excluding Social Security reform)	-$943	-$655	-$469	-$440	-$456	-$404
	-6.0%	-3.9%	-2.7%	-2.4%	-2.4%	-2.0%
Projected Deficit Under Plan (including Social Security reform)	-$949	-$646	-$455	-$421	-$432	-$372
	-$6.0%	-3.9%	-2.6%	-2.3%	-2.2%	-1.8%

Source: Report of the National Commission on Fiscal Responsibility and Reform (2010).
*Excludes Social Security.

Table 9.1. Simpson-Bowles Plan Summary

The president's bipartisan National Commission on Fiscal Responsibility and Reform submitted a report (Simpson-Bowles) proposing $2 of spending cuts for every $1 of tax revenue. That, along with savings in debt interest, would reduce the deficit by nearly $4 trillion, as summarized in *Table 9.1.*

2018	2019	2020	2012-2015	2012-2020	
$236	$261	$291	$464	$1,661	Discretionary Spending
$88	$97	$104	$134	$556	Mandatory Spending
$120	$150	$180	$140	$785	Spending in the Tax Code/Tax Reform
$36	$39	$43	$34	$210	Other Revenue
$119	$155	$199	$56	$673	Net Interest Savings
$599	$702	$817	$828	$3,885	Total Deficit Reduction*
-$332	-$343	-$333			Projected Deficit Under Plan (excluding Social Security reform)
-1.6%	-1.6%	-1.5%			
-$294	-$298	-$279			Projected Deficit Under Plan (including Social Security reform)
-1.4%	-1.3%	-1.2%			

Table 9.1. Simpson-Bowles Plan Summary

This plan would stabilize debt-to-GDP at 65% by 2020, eventually reducing it to a pre-crisis level of 40% by 2035.

In fact, if the U.S could come out of its current fiscal situation with only genuine tax reform (promoting work effort and growth), this would have a dramatic positive impact on the economy. According to Toder and Baneman (2010) of the Tax Policy Center, under one of the versions of the Simpson-Bowles proposal, average tax rates for higher-income groups increase while marginal tax rates for all income groups decline. Such a change in tax policy would have exactly the right effect on labor supply. Lower marginal tax rates would result in higher labor supply and, therefore, higher GDP.

On March 28, 2012, the House of Representatives overwhelmingly defeated the Simpson-Bowles Budget Resolution (382–38), an amendment introduced by U.S. Congressmen Jim Cooper (D-TN) and Steven LaTourette (R-OH). Apparently, neither the Republicans nor the Democrats were ready to embrace the Simpson-Bowles budget reform (e.g., eliminating deductions, lowering marginal tax rates, and decreasing entitlements).

Proposing to reduce the debt by $4 trillion, Simpson-Bowles offers an economically sound, bipartisan plan that would help restore the fiscal balance in the United States over the next 10 to 25 years.

The decisions Washington makes today will have a profound impact (for good or possibly for ill) on generations to come. America's financial crisis provides a rare opportunity to prevent economic catastrophe, and to put this nation on a path of common-sense fiscal reform.

APPENDIX

SIMPSON-BOWLES: KEY TAKE-AWAYS

In early 2010, President Obama appointed a blue-ribbon bipartisan panel to address the looming financial issues facing America. The panel consisted of 18 members, cochaired by Alan Simpson, the former Republican senator from Wyoming; and Erskine Bowles, chief of staff to President Clinton.[71] This resulted in The Moment of Truth, a report by the National Commission on Fiscal Responsibility and Reform(2010).

---

71 Commission members included: Bruce Reed, chief domestic policy adviser to President Clinton, serving as the executive director; and Sen. Max Baucus (D-MT); Rep. Xavier Becerra (D-CA); Rep. Dave Camp (R-MI); Sen. Tom Coburn (R-OK); Sen. Kent Conrad (D-ND); David Cote, chairman and CEO, Honeywell International; Sen. Mike Crapo (R-ID); Sen. Richard Durbin (D-IL); Ann Fudge, former CEO, Young & Rubicam Brands; Sen. Judd Gregg (R-NH); Rep. Jeb Hensarling (R-TX); Alice Rivlin, senior fellow, Brookings Institute, and former director, Office of Management & Budget; Rep. Paul Ryan (R-WI); Rep. Jan Schakowsky (D-IL); Rep. John Spratt (D-SC); and Andrew Stern, president, Service Employees International Union, serving as commissioners.

Eleven commission members supported the cochairs' report, and seven disagreed (a supermajority of fourteen votes was needed for the commission to formally endorse the fiscal blueprint for the government).

With federal spending in 2010 at about 24% of GDP and federal tax revenues at 15%, resulting in a deficit of about 9% of GDP and pushing the debt-to-GDP ratio to about 62%, Simpson-Bowles's mission was to achieve a $4 trillion reduction in budget deficits through 2020.

Commission members split into three working groups, with some overlap, to analyze discretionary spending, mandatory spending, and tax reform. The result was the six-part plan summarized below:

1. Discretionary Spending Cuts

The commission proposed to cap spending to achieve about a $1.760 trillion deficit reduction by 2020. Spending in 2012 was to be held at levels equal to or lower than spending in 2011, return to the pre-crisis level in 2013, and limit its growth to half that of inflation through 2020. These cuts and caps would come equally from the security and the nonsecurity parts of the discretionary budget, and be accompanied by procedural changes in Congress to raise the bar in enforcing them and requiring nonamendable tough votes in both chambers; restricting the use of emergency spending; fully funding transportation spending (rather than deficit spending) with a new 15-cent tax on gasoline; and mobilizing subcommittee resources in seeking ways to limit spending items, including congressional and White House spending.

2. Tax Reform

The goals of the tax reform included:

- Increase the tax base by eliminating loopholes, deductions, and tax spending

- Lower marginal income tax rate to spur economic activity

- Simplify the tax code

With the backdoor spending hidden in the tax code reduced or eliminated, a large increase would be expected in the tax base, allowing the country to reduce tax rates and simplify the tax code. *Table A.1* (which re-creates *Figure 6* in Simpson-Bowles) summarizes the gains in the tax rate reduction made possible by this fundamental tax reform.

	Bottom Rate		Middle Rate		Top Rate		Corporate Rate
Current Rates for 2010	10%	15%	25%	28%	33%	35%	35%
Scheduled Rates for 2011	15%		28%	31%	36%	39.6%	35%
Eliminate All Tax Expenditures	8%		14%		23%		26%
Keep Child Tax Credit + EITC	9%		15%		24%		26%
Enact Illustrative Tax Plan*	12%		22%		28%		28%

Source: Report of the National Commission on Fiscal Responsibility and Reform, December 2010.
*Dedicates $80 billion to deficit reduction in 2015 and taxes capital gains and dividends as ordinary income.

Table A.1. Tax rates under various scenarios

	Current Law	Illustrative Proposal (fully phased in)
Tax Rates for Individuals	In 2010, six brackets: 10% | 15% | 25% | 28% | 33% | 35% In 2011, five brackets: 15% | 28% | 31% | 36% | 39.6	Three brackets: 12% | 22% | 28%
Alternative Minimum Tax	Scheduled to hit middle-income individuals but "patched" annually	Permanently repealed
PEP and Pease	Repealed for 2010; resumes in 2011	Permanently repealed
EITC and Child Tax Credit	Partially refundable child tax credit of $1,000 per child. Refundable EITC of $457 to $5,666	Maintain current law of an equivalent alternative
Standard Deduction and Exemptions	Standard deduction of $5,700 ($11,400 for couple) for non-itemizers; personal and de-pendent exemptions of $3,650	Maintain current law; itemized deductions eliminated, so all individuals take standard deductions
Capital Gains and Dividends	In 2010, top rate of 15% for capital gains and dividends. In 2011, top rate of 20% for capital gains and dividends taxed as ordinary income	All capital gains and dividends taxed at ordinary income rates
Mortgage Interest	Deductible for itemizers. Mortgage capped at $1 million for principal and second resi-dences, plus an additional $100,000 for home equity	12% non-refundable tax credit available to all taxpayers. Mortgage capped at $500,000. No credit for interest from second residence and equity
Employer-Provided Health Care Insurance	Excluded from income. 40% excise tax on high-cost plans (generally $27,500 for families) begins in 2018; threshold indexed to inflation	Exclusion capped at 75th percen-tile of premium levels in 2014, with cap frozen in normal terms through 2018 and phased out by 2038. Excise tax reduced to 12%
Charitable Giving	Deductible for itemizers	12% non-refundable tax credit available to all taxpayers; available above 2% of Adjusted Gross Income (AGI) floor
State and Municipal Bonds	Interest exempt from income	Interest taxable as income for newly issued bonds
Retirement	Multiple retirement account options with different contribution limits; saver's credit of up to $1,000	Consolidate retirement accounts; cap tax-preferred contributions to lower of $20,000 or 20% of income, expand saver's credit
Other Tax Expenditures	Over 150 additional tax expenditures	Nearly all other income tax expenditures are eliminated

Source: Report of the National Commission on Fiscal Responsibility and Reform, December 2010.

Table A.2. Illustrative Individual Tax Reform Plan

178

Table A.2 (which re-creates Simpson-Bowles *Figure.7*) describes the reforms that reduce or eliminate tax spending.

According to Toder and Baneman (2010) of the Tax Policy Center, the proposed tax reforms would result in a slightly more progressive tax system, in the sense that the top quintile in the population would experience the largest increase in their average income tax rate.

Part of the tax reform called for the elimination of all tax expenditures for businesses. Removing these artificial and political favors would extend the corporate income tax base sufficiently to allow a reduction in the corporate income tax rate and make American companies more competitive worldwide.

3. Health Care Savings

The projected increase in future health expenditures is the single most important reason for the fiscal imbalance. As a result, the commission made specific proposals to contain these expenditures and save about $400 billion through 2020.

In 1997, the "sustainable growth rate" (SGR), also known as the "doc fix," was created to control Medicare spending by setting payment targets on doctors' fees and reducing these physician service fees if spending exceeded targets. The SGR led to a reduction in physician salaries in 2002. However, Congress blocked the reductions in 2003 and has done so each successive year since then. Simpson-Bowles proposes to freeze payments at the 2012 levels, but this would still cost about $267 billion relative to current law that would have to be financed by savings in other areas of the health system.

A second proposal for health care is to reform or repeal the Community Living Assistance Services and Supports (CLASS)

Act, which established a voluntary long-term-care insurance program enacted as part of the Affordable Care Act (ACA). Although the program addressed an important public policy concern—the need for noninstitutional long-term care—it is not financially sound. However, repealing it would raise costs, since the premiums are collected up front, with expenditures to be forthcoming.

The third and key component of the health care savings portion of Simpson-Bowles proposes a large number of Medicare, Medicaid, and other savings to more than pay for the SGR and CLASS proposals above. Among the measures to achieve savings suggested are:

- Increase government authority and funding to reduce Medicare fraud

- Reform Medicare cost-sharing rules

- Restrict first-dollar coverage in Medicare supplemental insurance

- Extend Medicaid drug rebates to dual eligibles (individuals who are also eligible for Medicare)

- Reduce excess payments to hospitals for medical education

- Cut Medicare payments for bad debts

- Accelerate home health savings in the ACA

- Eliminate state gaming of Medicaid tax gimmick

- Place dual eligibles in Medicaid managed care

- Reduce funding for Medicaid administrative costs

- Allow expedited application for Medicaid waivers in well-qualified states

- Reform medical malpractice

4. Other Mandatory Policies

Mandatory programs other than Social Security, Medicare, and Medicaid make up slightly less than one-fifth of the federal budget. These programs include federal civilian and military retirement, income support programs, veterans' benefits, agricultural subsidies, student loans, and others.

For example, reforming federal workforce retirement programs would be expected to save about $70 billion over 10 years. Reducing agricultural spending programs would save about $10 billion over 8 years, whereas eliminating in-school subsidies in federal student loan programs would save $43 billion.

Bend Point Locations in 2010	Current Law	Proposal	Projected Bend Point Locations in 2050 (in 2010 Dollars)
$0 to $9,000	90%	90%	$0 to $15,000
$9,000 to $38,000	32%	30%	$15,000 to $63,000
$38,000 to $64,000		10%	$63,000 to $102,000
$64,000 to $107,000	15%	5%	$102,000 to $173,000
>$107,000	n/a		$173,000 to tax max

Source: Report of the National Commission on Fiscal Responsibility and Reform, December 2010.
Note: All numbers are FC staff-estimated and rounded to the nearest $1,000.

Table A.3. Social Security Bend Points

5. Social Security

Apart from some proposals to protect the extremely old and poorest retirees, Simpson-Bowles proposes four key reforms to the current Social Security system. First, the benefit formula would change to a slightly more progressive formula by splitting the middle bracket into two brackets in an attempt to contain future costs. *Table A.3* (which re-creates Simpson-Bowles *Figure 11*) describes the current versus the proposed formulas.

Second, Simpson-Bowles proposes to gradually increase both the early retirement age (ERA) and the normal retirement age (NRA). Indexing both to increases in life expectancy would raise the ERA and NRA to 64 and 69, respectively, in 2075.

Third, the commission proposed to raise the maximum taxable income gradually to cover 90% of wages by 2050.

Fourth, the report proposes to mandate coverage to newly hired state and local employees by 2020. This would create new revenue for the federal program and also relieve state and local governments from unsustainable future retirement liabilities.

6. Process Reform

Finally, Simpson-Bowles urges the federal government to streamline various processes for measuring inflation better for indexed provisions, establish procedures to enforce reduction targets, and review and reform budget concepts.

In summary, the cochairs' report makes significant concrete proposals on both spending and taxation that lead to a much lower debt-to-GDP ratio by 2040.

REFERENCES

Alesina, Alberto, Silva Ardagna, Roberto Perotti and Fabio Schiantarelli. 2002. "Fiscal Policy, Profits, and Investment." *The American Economic Review,* 92 (3): 571–89.

Auerbach, Alan J. 2009. "Long-Term Objectives for Government Debt." *FinanzArchiv: Public Finance Analysis, Mohr Siebeck, Tübingen,* 65 (4): 472-501. http://ideas.repec.org/a/mhr/finarc/urnsici0015-2218(200912)654_472lofgd_2.0.tx_2-t.html.

Baicker, Katherine and Jonathan S. Skinner. 2011. "Health Care Spending Growth and the Future of U.S. Tax Rates." NBER Working Paper No. 16772.

Barro, Robert J. 1991. "Economic Growth in a Cross Section of Countries," *The Quarterly Journal of Economics,* 106 (2): 407–43.

Office of Management and Budget. 2012. *Analytical Perspectives. Budget of the U.S. Government, Fiscal 2013.* http://www.whitehouse.gov/sites/default/files/omb/budget/fy2013/assets/spec.pdf.

Bureau of Economic Analysis, U.S. Department of Commerce. 2011. National Income and Product Accounts (NIPA): Table 3.15.5. [http://www.bea.gov.]

Bureau of Economic Analysis, U.S. Department of Commerce. 2012. National Income and Product Accounts (NIPA): Tables 1.1.1, 1.1.5, 3.1, 3.2, 3.3, 3.12, 3.15.5, 3.18, 5.10U. [http://www.bea.gov.].

Chamley, Christophe. 1986. "Optimal Taxation of Capital Income in General Equilibrium with Infinite Lives." *Econometrica,* 54 (3): 607–22.

Chen, Kaiji and Ayse Imrohoroglu. 2012. "Debt and the U.S. Economy." Working paper, USC.

Chetty, Raj, Adam Guren, Dayanand S. Manoli, and Andrea Weber. 2011. "Does Indivisible Labor Explain the Difference Between Micro and Macro Elasticities? A Meta-Analysis of Extensive Margin Elasticities." NBER Working Paper No. 16729. http://www.nber.org/papers/w16729.

Cogan, John F., R. Glenn Hubbard, and Daniel P. Kessler. 2011. *Healthy, Wealthy, & Wise: 5 Steps to a Better Healthcare System,* 2nd ed. Stanford, Calif.: Hoover Institution Press; Washington, D.C.: AEI Press.

Congressional Budget Office. 2008. *Key Issues in Analyzing Major Health Insurance Proposals, December 2008.* http://www.cbo.gov/ftpdocs/99xx doc9924/toc.shtml.

Congressional Budget Office. 2011a. *CBO's 2011 Long-Term Budget Outlook* (including Supplemental Data), June. http://www.cbo.gov/doc.cfm?index=12212.

Congressional Budget Office. 2011b. "CBO's Role in the Budget Process."http://www.cbo.gov/aboutcbo/budgetprocess.cfm.

Congressional Budget Office. 2011c. Letter from Douglas W. Elmendorf, Director, Congressional Budget Office to John A. Boehner, Speaker, U.S. House of Representatives and Honorable Harry Reid, Majority Leader, United States Senate, with attachments, August. http://www.cbo.gov/ftpdocs/123xx/doc12357/BudgetControlActAug1.

Cutler, David M. 2004. *Your Money or Your Life: Strong Medicine for America's Health Care System.* New York: Oxford University Press.

Davis, S. J. and M. Henrekson. 2005. "Tax Effects on Work Activity, Industry Mix and Shadow Economy Size: Evidence from Rich-Country Comparisons." In *Labour Supply and Incentives to Work in Europe,* edited by Goméz-Salvador, R., A. Lamo, B. Petrongolo, M. Ward, and E. Wasmer. 44–104. Northampton, Mass.: Edward Elgar Press.

De Nardi, Mariacristina, Selahattin Imrohoroglu, and Thomas J. Sargent. 1999. "Projected U.S. Demographics and Social Security," *Review of Economic Dynamics,* 2 (3): 575–615.

Toder, Eric, and Daniel Baneman. 2010. "UPDATED: Distributional Estimates for Several Variants of Option 1 of the Bowles-Simpson "Chairmen's Mark,"" Tax Policy Center. Urban Institute and Brookings Institution. http://taxpolicycenter.org/taxtopics/bowles-simpson.cfm.

Feldstein, Martin, and Daniel Feenberg. 1995. "The Effect of Increased Tax Rates on Taxable Income and Economic Efficiency: A Preliminary Analysis of the 1993 Tax Rate Increases," NBER Working Paper 5370.

Feldstein, Martin. 2006. "The Effect of Taxes on Efficiency and Growth," *Tax Notes* 111 (6): 679–84.

Fölster, Stefan and Magnus Henrekson. 2001. "Growth Effects of Government Expenditure and Taxation in Rich Countries," *European Economic Review,* 45 (8): 1501–20.

Garber, Alan M. 2008. "A Menu Without Prices," Annals of Internal Medicine, 148 (12): 964–-6.

Giavazzi, Francesco and Marco Pagano. 1990. "Can Severe Fiscal Contractions Be Expansionary? Tales of Two Small European Countries.," *NBER Macroeconomics Annual 1990,* edited by d.Olivier Jean Blanchard and Stanley Fischer. (5):75-122. Cambridge, Mass.: MIT Press.

Grayson, Vincent K. and Victoria A. Velkoff. 2010. "The Next Four Decades. The Older Population in the United States: 2010 to 2050," U.S. Department of Commerce. U.S. Census Bureau.

The Groningen Growth and Development Center (GGDC). http://www.rug.nl/feb/onderzoek/onderzoekscentra/ggdc/index.

Hadley, Jack, John Holahan, Teresa Coughlin, and Dawn Miller. 2008. "Covering the Uninsured in 2008: Current Costs, Sources of Payment, and Incremental Costs," *Health Affairs,* 27 (5): w399–w415.

Hall, Robert E. and Charles I. Jones. 2007. "The Value of Life and the Rise in Health Spending." *The Quarterly Journal of Economics,* 122 (1): 39–72.

Imrohoroglu, Selahattin and Sagiri Kitao. 2011. "Social Security Reforms: Benefit Claiming, Labor Force Participation, and Long-run Sustainability," Working Paper, University of Southern California.

Jones, Charles I. and Peter J. Klenow. 2009. "Beyond GDP? Welfare Across Countries and Time," Working Paper, Stanford University.

Judd, Kenneth. 1985. "Redistributive taxation in a simple perfect foresight model." *Journal of Public Economics,* 28: 59–83.

Kessler, Daniel and Mark McClellan. 1996. "Do doctors practice defensive medicine?" *The Quarterly Journal of Economics*, 111 (2): 353–90.

Lawver, Daniel. 2010. "Measuring quality increases in the medical sector," Working paper. Arizona State University.

Ljungqvist, Lars and Thomas J. Sargent. 2006. "Do Taxes Explain European Employment? Indivisible Labor, Human Capital, Lotteries, and Savings?" In *NBER Macroeconomics Annual 2006, Volume 21,* edited by Acemoglu, D., K. Rogoff, and M. Woodford. 181–246. Cambridge, Mass.: MIT Press.

Lucas, Robert E. 1990. "Supply-side economics: An analytical review." *Oxford Economic Papers,* 42 (2): 293–316.

McDaniel, Cara. 2011. " Average tax rates on consumption, investment, labor, and capital in the OECD 1950–-2003."Arizona State University. Extended data: http://www.caramcdaniel.com/.

Maddison, Angus. 2010. *Historical Statistics of the World Economy: 1–2008 AD*, Tables 2 and 3. http://www.ggdc.net/.

McKinsey Global Institute. 2008. *Accounting for the cost of US health care: A new look at why Americans spend more.* McKinsey & Company. http://www.mckinsey.com/mgi/reports/pdfs/healthcare/US_healthcare_report.pdf.

Murphy, Kevin M. and Robert H. Topel. 2006. "The Value of Health and Longevity." *Journal of Public Economy*, 114 (5): 871-904.

National Health Expenditures, 2010 Highlights, Centers for Medicare and Medicaid Services. [http://www.cms.gov/Research-Statistics-Data-and-Systems/Statistics-Trends-and-Reports/NationalHealthExpendData/downloads//highlights.pdf]

Newhouse, Joseph P. 1992. "Medical Care Costs: How Much Welfare Loss?" *The Journal of Economic Perspectives*, 6 (3): 3–21.

OECD. 2011a. "*Government at a Glance 2011*", OECD Publishing. doi: 10.1787/gov_glance-2011-en.

OECD. 2011b. "From gross public to total net social spending, 2007." (Table 2007fc-e27), *OECD Social Expenditures Database (SOCX)*. [http://www.oecd.org/els/social/expenditure.]

OECD. 2011c. *OECD Health Data 201,1, 30 June 30, 2011.*, Llast updated: July 21, 2011., Ddata extracted on 06 September 6, 2011. [hhttp://www.oecd.org/document/16/0,3746,en_2649_34631_2085200_1_1_1,00.html.]

OECD. 2012. Economic Outlook 90 database, Annex Tables 27 and 33. http://www.oecd.org/document/61/0,3746,en_2649_34109_2483901_1_1_1,00.html.

OECD.Stat. 2011a. Annual National Accounts, Government Accounts, Dataset 11: Government Expenditure by Function. Data extracted on April 8, 2011. http://stats.oecd.org/WBOS/index.aspx

OECD.Stat. 2011b. Annual National Accounts, Main Aggregates, Dataset 1: Gross Domestic Product. Data extracted on April 8, 2011. http://stats.oecd.org/Index.aspx?DatasetCode=SNA_TABLE1.

OECD.StatExtracts. 2011a. Revenue Statistics – Comparative Tables, Total Government, Tax Rrevenue as Ppercentage of GDP., Ddata extracted on 06 April 6, 2011. [http://stats.oecd.org/Index.aspx?DataSetCode=REV.]

OECD.StatExtracts. 2011b. Labor Force Statistics (MEI). [http://stats.oecd.org/index.aspx?DatasetCode=MEILABOUR.]

OECD.StatExtracts. 2011ca. Health. Health Care Resources: Remuneration of health professionals., Ddata extracted on 06 September 6, 2011. [http://stats.oecd.org/Index.aspx?DataSetCode=SHA.]

Ohanian, Lee, Andrea Raffo, and Richard Rogerson. 2008. "Long-Term Changes in Labor Supply and Taxes: Evidence from OECD Countries 1956–2004." *Journal of Monetary Economics* 5(8): 1353–1362.

Office of Management and Budget. 2012a. *Fiscal Year 2012 Historical Tables Budget of the U.S. Government*, Washington, D.C.A: U.S. Government Printing Office. http://www.whitehouse.gov/omb/budget/Historicals.

Office of Management and Budget. 2011b. "Special Topics, 18. Aid to State and Local Governments." *Analytical Perspectives, Budget of the United States Government, Fiscal Year 2012*. http://www.whitehouse.gov/sites/default/files/omb/budget/fy2012/assets/topics.pdf.

Prescott, Edward. 2004. "Why Do Americans Work So Much More Than Europeans?" *Federal Reserve Bank of Minneapolis Quarterly Review*, 28 (1): 2–13.

Ragan, Kelly. 2005. "Taxes, Transfers and Time Use: Fiscal Policy in a Household Production Model." Chicago: Mimeo, University of Chicago.

Reinhart, C. M. and K. S. Rogoff. 2010. "Growth in a Time of Debt," *American Economic Review*, American Economic Association, 100 (2): May, 573–78.

Reinhardt, Uwe E., Peter S. Hussey, and Gerard F. Anderson. 2002. "Cross-National Comparisons of Health Systems Using OECD Data, 1999." *Health Affairs*, 21 (3): 169–181.

Rogerson, Richard. 2007. "Taxation and Market Work: Is Scandinavia an Outlier?" *Economic Theory*, 32 (1): 59–85.

Rogerson, Richard. 2006. "Understanding Differences in Hours Worked." *Review of Economic Dynamics*, 9 (3): 365–409.

Rogerson, Richard and Johanna Wallenius. 2009. "Micro and Macro Elasticities in a Life Cycle Model with Taxes." *Journal of Economic Theory*, 144 (6): 2277–2292.

Suen, Richard M. H. 2006. "Technological Advance and the Growth in Health Care Spending." Working Paper, University of California, Riverside.

The Federal Reserve Bank of Minneapolis, "The Recession and Recovery in Perspective." [http://www.minneapolisfed.org/publications_papers/studies/recession_perspective/index.cfm].

The National Commission on Fiscal Responsibility and Reform. 2010. "The Moment of Truth: Report of the National Commission on Fiscal Responsibility and Reform." http://www.fiscalcommission.gov/sites/fiscalcommission.gov/files/documents/TheMomentofTruth12_1_2010.pdf.

U.S. Department of the Treasury. 2011a. Financial Management Service. *Treasury Bulletin*, September. Federal Debt, Table FD-1. http://www.fms.treas.gov/bulletin/index.html.

U.S. Department of the Treasury. 2011b. "U.S. Treasury-Foreign Holdings of U.S. Debt," Treasury International Capital System (TIC)–Home Page. http://www.treasury.gov/resource-center/data-chart-center/tic/Documents/mfh.txt.

U.S. Department of the Treasury, Internal Revenue Service. 2011c. Publication 15, (Circular E), Employer's Tax Guide. http://www.irs.gov/pub/irs-pdf/p15.pdf.

Weinstein, Milton C. and Jonathan S. Skinner. 2010. "Comparative Effectiveness and Health Care Spending—Implications for Reform." *New England Journal of Medicine*, 362: 460–465.

Woolhandler, S., T. Campbell, and D. U. Himmelstein. 2003. "Costs of Health Care Administration in the U.S. and Canada," *New England Journal of Medicine*, August 21, 349 (TK issue number): 768–75.

FIGURES

Figure 3.1: Maddison (2010).
Figure 3.2: Bureau of Economic Analysis (2011). NIPA Table 1.1.1.
Figure 3.3: Maddison (2010).
Figure 3.4: Maddison (2010).
Figure 3.5: Maddison (2010).
Figure 4.1: Office of Management and Budget (2012a). Table 1.2.
Figure 4.2: Office of Management and Budget (2012a). Table 7.1.
Figure 4.3: OECD (2012d). Annex Table 33.
Table 4.1: Bureau of Economic Analysis (2012). NIPA Tables 3.1, 3.2, 3.3.
Figure 4.4: Bureau of Economic Analysis (2011). NIPA Table 3.15.5.
Figure 4.5: Bureau of Economic Analysis (2012). NIPA Tables 1.1.5 and 3.1.
Figure 4.6: Bureau of Economic Analysis (2012). NIPA Table 3.15.5.
Figure 4.7: Bureau of Economic Analysis (2012). NIPA Tables 1.1.5 and 3.2.
Figure 4.8: OECD.Stat (2011a, 2011b). Dataset 1 and 11.
Figure 4.9: OECD.Stat (2011a, 2011b). Dataset 1 and 11.
Figure 4.10: OECD.Stat (2011a, 2011b). Dataset 1 and 11.
Figure 4.11:OECD (2011b). Table 2007fc−e27.
Table 5.1: Bureau of Economic Analysis (2012). NIPA Tables 1.1.5 and 3.1.
Table 5.2: Bureau of Economic Analysis (2012). NIPA Tables 3.2 and 3.3.
Figure 5.1: Bureau of Economic Analysis (2012). NIPA Table 3.1.
Figure 5.2: Bureau of Economic Analysis (2011). NIPA Tables 3.1 and 3.2.
Figure 5.3: OECD.StatExtracts (2011a).
Table 6.1: Prescott (2004).
Figure 6.1: Prescott (2004).
Figure 6.2: OECD.StatExtracts (2011b).
Figure 6.3: McDaniel (2011).
Table 6.2: McDaniel (2011).
Table 6.3: U.S. Department of Treasury (2011b).
Table 6.4: Reinhart and Rogoff (2010).
Figure 7.1: Congressional Budget Office (2011a).
Figure 7.2: Congressional Budget Office (2011a).
Figure 7.3: Congressional Budget Office (2011a).
Figure 7.4: Congressional Budget Office (2011a).
Table 7.1: Authors' calculations.
Figure 7.5: Authors' calculations.
Figure 7.6: Authors' calculations.
Figure 7.7: Authors' calculations.
Figure 7.8: Congressional Budget Office (2011a) and authors' calculations.
Figure 8.1: Congressional Budget Office (2011a).
Figure 8.2: Centers for Medicare & Medicaid Services (2010).
Figure 8.3: Congressional Budget Office (2011a).
Figure 8.4: OECD (2011b).
Figure 8.5: OECD (2011b).
Figure 8.6: OECD (2011c).
Figure 8.7: OECD (2011b).
Table 8.1: Reinhardt, Hussey, and Anderson (2002).
Figure 8.8: OECD.StatExtracts (2011c).
Figure 8.9: OECD.StatExtracts (2011c).
Figure 9.1: Federal Reserve Bank of Minneapolis.
Table 9.1: National Commission on Fiscal Responsibility and Reform (2010).
Table A1: National Commission on Fiscal Responsibility and Reform (2010).
Table A2: National Commission on Fiscal Responsibility and Reform (2010).
Table A3: National Commission on Fiscal Responsibility and Reform (2010).

ACKNOWLEDGEMENTS

We would like to express our gratitude to our mentors, colleagues, and friends at the University of Minnesota who taught us Minnesota economics. Special thanks go to Edward C. Prescott, Nobel laureate 2004, and Thomas J. Sargent, Nobel laureate 2011, for continued guidance and encouragement throughout our professional lives.

We would also like to thank Joe Ricketts for giving us an opportunity to think about how to use our knowledge and make an important point. This book would not have been possible without his concern and passion for improving the future of the American economy.

Thanks to Webster Stone, our editor, who worked tirelessly to improve the manuscript, in terms of both style and readability, and Dr. Mukesh Bajaj, our advisory editor, as well as Dr. Kelly Nordby, and Urmi Mukherjea for all their help.

THE AUTHORS

Ayşe İmrohoroğlu is a professor of finance and business economics at the University of Southern California's Marshall School of Business, where she has served as chair of the Finance and Business Economics Department. She specializes in business cycles, inflation, unemployment insurance, and Social Security. She is also an editor of the *European Economic Review*.

Selahattin İmrohoroğlu is a professor of finance and business economics at the University of Southern California's Marshall School of Business, where he is the academic director and assistant dean of the IBEAR MBA program. He specializes in taxes, savings, and Social Security.